TAL: Location and History

TAL: Location and History

Regaining Lost Ground

GIDEON BAKLIT

Edited by Professor Monday Y. Mangvwat
Department of History and International Studies,
University of Jos, Nigeria

authorHOUSE®

AuthorHouse™ UK
1663 Liberty Drive
Bloomington, IN 47403 USA
www.authorhouse.co.uk
Phone: 0800.197.4150

Published by AuthorHouse   03/23/2015

ISBN: 978-1-4918-9742-3 (sc)
ISBN: 978-1-4918-9743-0 (hc)
ISBN: 978-1-4918-9744-7 (e)

Print information available on the last page.

Any people depicted in stock imagery provided by Thinkstock are models,
and such images are being used for illustrative purposes only.
Certain stock imagery © Thinkstock.

This book is printed on acid-free paper.

Contents

LIST OF TABLES

LIST OF FIGURES

Principal Authors

- Gideon Baklit, Associate Professor, University of Jos, Nigeria
- Dr Charles C. Jacob (former member staff of history department, University of Jos, Nigeria)

Research Team

- Dr Everestus G. Yanan (Late)
- Ayo. E. Dangway
- Istifanus Bakwai

Contributors

- Mr Bala Rumtong
- Mrs Laraba Mudutgap
- Reverend Bulus Tsetu (Late)
- CSP Andrew Gabkwet (Rtd.)
- Chief E. L. Youbamson (Ngollong Tal, Jos)

This book is dedicated to the people of Tal at home or in the Diaspora, and in recognition of our dearly beloved friends and brothers, the late Reverend Bulus Tsetu and Dr Everestus.

G. Yanan

Foreword

This book is a fascinating account of several important themes on Tal geography, history, agriculture, religion, arts, culture, science, and technology. Several experts from various academic disciplines contributed to this work, adding to its fascination and strength. The main researcher, Gideon Baklit, and his colleague, the late Charles C. Jacobs, are well-known scholars. The former is a geographer, while the latter was a historian with training in social anthropology. The two have blended together to produce a pioneering study of the cultural ecology of Tal society through time in a thrilling and captivating manner.

When Gideon Baklit requested me to peruse an earlier draft of the book, I gladly accepted the task for two main reasons. Firstly, the Tal people, a small community on Nigeria's Jos Plateau, have been described in the colonial literature as "stubborn," "truculent," "violent," "cannibalistic," and independent-minded; the community exhibits a morbid hatred for authority, a description that applied to almost all Jos Plateau communities, which provided an alibi for the extreme brutality meted out during the colonial conquest. But the brutality in Tal was overblown beyond reasonable proportions on account of the murder of Lankuk, a colonial Ngas paramount chief, while on tour of Tal District in 1917. Lankuk, along with his entire entourage of fifty-two people, were murdered by the Tal people. The Tal version of that sordid episode is now available to the public.

This book is an important addition to the recently growing stock of literature on the various ethnic nationalities on the Jos Plateau, something that has been going on for decades on Hausa land, Yoruba land, Igbo land, and Delta communities. Indeed, with similar studies on the other Jos Plateau groups such as the Ngas, Mwaghavul, Berom, Afizere, Goemai, Tarok, and Pengana, the Nigerian minority ethnic nationalities, largely located in central Nigeria, this is a clear response to Hogdkin's dilemma on the historiography of these Nigerian minority groups. For in defending why his invaluable anthology had no entries on the communities of the Nigerian middle belt, including the Jos Plateau, Hogdkin wrote:

I admit paying too little attention to several interesting secondary Themes—the histories of the Tiv, Idoma, Igala, Igbirra, among others. This neglect is not something which I can honestly try to justify except on grounds of shortage of space, time, and knowledge. I am conscious that excellent anthologies could be constructed—and no doubt will be around the histories of the various peoples who appear too rarely, or not at all, in this one.[1]

And so I excitedly read through the first draft and made corrections. I also drew the attention of Gideon Baklit to certain archival sources to enrich the book, and I made other suggestions which he gladly accepted. I am happy that these have been done and the book is now a remarkably improved version of the earlier draft. To the best of my knowledge, this is an original and pioneering study of Tal history and culture which academic researchers and policy makers alike would find very useful. Local or native words and names are rendered as such but translated where necessary, assisted by appropriate sketches, plates, and pictures. These have enormously aided the non-Tal researcher and reader.

This is an original and pioneering book, and I am sure that the authors would welcome reviews and criticisms of it so that any shortcomings that might be taken care of in a subsequent edition. As one who has "midwifed" and refereed several similar publications on the Jos Plateau, this book is as good as the others and a welcomed development. I therefore commend it to students of history, geography, culture, and religion, not just on the Jos Plateau but throughout Nigeria, Africa, and beyond. Needless to say, Tal speakers must be most delighted at the appearance of this fascinating account of their rich history.

Professor Monday Yakiban Mangvwat

Department of History and International Studies

University of Jos, Nigeria

---

[1]   Thomas Hodgkin, *Nigerian Perspectives: An Historical Anthology*. London, New York: Oxford University Press, 1975, pp. 3-4.

Acknowledgement

I wish to acknowledge the immense contributions of the Tal Community Development Association (TCDA), His Royal Highness, Ambrose Gupiya, District Head of Tal, E. D. Dangway, Yakubu Mitok (late), John Guwan (former deputy chairman, Pankshin LGA), and Group Captain Danladi Y. Baltu, who gave his Peugeot 504 car free of charge for the research trips to Tal with late Dr Charles C. Jacob.

My special words of appreciation go to my former vice chancellor of the University of Jos, Professor Monday Mangvwat, who agreed to edit the work on short notice. In fact, I am highly delighted because his professional touch made a significant impact on the quality of the book. I also want to acknowledge the contributions of Reverend LaVonna Ennis and Reverend Scott Enis, USA, for editing the original draft given to them by late Reverend Bulus Tsetu. They did it free of charge and ensured that the work was completed and returned to us for further action.

Chapter One

Introduction

1.1 Location, Land Size, and People

Tal is a geo-political entity as well as the language of a people, located in the south-eastern part of Pankshin Local Government Area in Plateau State, Nigeria. It has a land size of about 104 square miles (Ames, 1934, p. 125).

Tal is one of the oldest districts created by the British colonial masters in the former Pankshin Division (now Local Government Area), comprised of twenty-two villages or hamlets (Langan, Pankshin Divisional Office, 1945). The district headquarters is Balong. It was established around 1914 by Mutkhai as a result of trading activities with Hausa people, who came from Bauchi and Katsina. Articles of trade were silk, cotton, groundnuts, kola nuts, guinea corn, and beans. This was done through trade by barter. The original villages were Kwopzak, Hamtul, Kabwai, Tangge, Basnuang, Takhong, Khongbalam, Mungne, Mudong, Khongkhol, Khongbwong, Wettal, Zemsu, Kyam, Yong, Kwaklak, Kabiyak, Damhi, Dasuk, Kajop, Gosol, and Dhan. The district is bounded to the south by Piapung (Mikang LGA), to the west by Chip (Pankshin LGA), to the east by Pai (Pankshin), and to the north by Garram (Kanke LGA).

Tal is an Angas tribe (Temple, 1965), named after the district they occupy. Though akin to Ngas, it is difficult to ascertain their ethnic connections and variation. Although they both claim Bornu as their place of origin, Tal people have a unique dialect and speak a different language from Angas, semi-Bantu class, and they do not circumcise (Ames, 1934, p. 148). In terms of communication, now Tal can easily be accessed with the recent introduction of GSM. Meek (1971) classified Tal with Chip and Angas in the Bornu sub-section of the Benue-Chad group of Sudanese languages.

1

The sacred cults and objects of the Tal are similar to those of the Angas. For example, both groups use *Nwong, Tau, Fwan*, and *Yer*. They have also adapted religious symbols from other ethnic groups.

1.2 Physical Features

Relief

The Tal area tends to maintain geographical contiguity. The district is hilly with abrupt escarpments and narrow intervening (resonant) valley systems. Near Mudong, the land rises from 2,000 feet to a height of over 4,000 feet above sea level (Buchanan and Pugh, 1971). There is a valley running west of Kwopzak into Muri (Jalingo). Plains divide the district into two well-defined areas with a steep ascent on either side. On the western side of the district, the mountains slope more gradually. The whole area is dissected into a series of steep spurs and narrow valleys. The Tal district forms a part of the mountains rising out of Muri (Jalingo) plains. It is cut off from the Angas Mountains by the valley that runs from Garram (Kanke LGA) in a south-westerly direction by Buzuk into Jalingo plains and by the low ground lying south and east of Garram (see Figure 1.1).

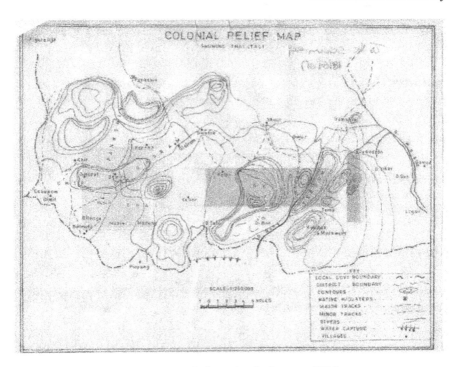

Figure 1.1: Colonial relief map of Tal

The average height of the district is between 2,000 and 3,000 feet above sea level (Kowal and Knabe, 1972). The rock type belongs to the Precambrian basement class and consists of high and low grades of metamorphic and igneous rocks. The complex soils are ferruginous tropical soil on crystalline rocks and lithosols (Kowal and Knabe, 1972). Weathered rocks produce large quantities of regolith materials, which are rich in sand and clay in many parts of the district (Baklit, 1984).

The Rivers Wase and Shimankar drain the area (figure 1.1.). Thus, Tal district lies within the watershed of these two river systems that flow southwards to join the River Benue. They are perennial, while some of their tributaries are ephemeral, with a tendency towards water levels suddenly rising during the wet season and reducing or even drying up during the dry season.

Vegetation

A broad vegetal cover of Tal district is the Northern Guinea Savannah. Natural vegetation has been greatly tampered with due to extensive socio-economic activities. Consequently, modified vegetation exists with patches of natural vegetation on hill slopes. There is a gallery of forest cover along the river valleys or channels and much uncultivated bush in hilly areas. This consists of shrubs, herbs, and short grasses. Within cultivated settlement patterns, economic trees, such as locust beans, silk cotton, baobab, mango, and *borasus* (desert palm), abound.

Climate

Tal district experiences mostly relief rainfall. Mean annual rainfall is about 1,143 centimetres (Resource Study Paper No. 29, 1978). Kowal and Knabe (1972) put it at between forty-five and fifty inches. The length of rainy season is approximately 190 to 200 days. There are two marked seasons:

(1) dry season, which starts at the end of October and lasts till March
(2) rainy season, which spans from the 1st to the 10th of April and ends in October (11th to 20th)

The global change in weather has caused these seasons to fluctuate. The average mean temperature is between 68 and 90 degrees F (Federal Surveys, 1964).

Being in the southern part of Plateau escarpments, these characteristics of well-marked seasons apply:

(i)   a cool dry winter (December-February)
(ii)   a hot dry spring (March-May)
(iii) a warm wet season (June-August)
(iv)   a less well-marked season (September-November), with decreasing rainfall

1.3 Population

The people of Tal are not a large group. Records of their numbers over the years have been difficult to obtain due to several factors.

Table 1.1 Population of Tal, from Colonial Period to 1991-2006

S/N	Year	Number
1	1917	17,000
2	1934	9,140
3	1934-39	9,343
4	1945-46	8,444
5	1963	8,735
6	1965	12,200
7	1991	26,235

Table 1.1 shows that the population of Tal was 17,000 in 1917. It dropped to 8,735 in 1963 but increased in 1965 to 12,200 and to 26,235 in 1991. The 1991 census, table 1.2, shows the population of Tal projected up to 2016 by locality.

Given the projected population, by 2012 Puyam would have up to 2,000 people, Kabwai, Hamtul, Kyam, and Tangge population will have less than 2,000, while places like Lapmwa, Gyen, and Dumbi had ess than 500 people.

1.4 Transportation and Communication

Transportation and communication with the outside world is very difficult. There is no good road linking the district to the nearest town. Only one poorly constructed dry season road links Tal with Baban Lamba, joining Panyam-Shendam Jos via a tarred road. There is a second seasonal road from Tal to Garram to Sharam-Kabwir (Kanke LGA) that links Pankshi-Shendam. Again, this is not very motorable or accessible. Thus, movement of people, goods, and services, as wells as communication and social interaction, are very difficult.

Table 1.2: Projected Population of Tal by Locality 1991-2016

S/N	Locality	1991			1996			2001			2006			2011			2016		
		M	F	Total	M	F	Total	M	F	Total	M	F	Total	M	F	Total	M	F	Total
1	Kongballam	165	178	343	188	203	391	274	257	531	266	308	575	296	342	638	325	376	702
2	Basnuang	185	203	388	211	231	442	307	293	600	299	351	650	332	390	722	365	429	794
3	Puyam	486	550	1036	554	627	1181	807	794	1600	785	952	1738	872	1057	1929	959	1163	2122
4	Kabwai	245	261	506	279	298	577	407	377	783	396	452	848	439	502	941	483	552	1035
5	Hamtul	277	252	529	316	287	603	460	364	823	448	436	884	497	484	981	547	533	1079
6	Dasuk	191	221	412	218	252	470	317	319	636	309	383	691	343	425	767	377	467	844
7	Kobzak	423	497	920	482	567	1049	702	717	1419	684	860	1544	759	955	1714	835	1051	1885
8	Gung	171	162	333	195	185	380	284	234	518	276	280	557	307	311	618	337	342	680
9	Dumbi/Others	79	100	179	90	114	204	131	144	275	128	173	301	142	192	334	156	211	367
10	Kwashi	153	189	342	174	215	390	254	273	527	247	327	574	274	363	638	302	400	701
11	Lampmwa	58	58	116	66	66	132	96	84	180	94	100	194	104	111	215	114	123	237
12	Kyam/Others	508	353	861	579	402	982	843	509	1353	821	611	1432	911	678	1590	1002	746	1749
13	Kwali	124	128	252	141	146	287	206	185	390	200	222	422	222	246	468	245	271	515
14	Gyen	78	65	143	89	74	163	129	94	223	126	113	239	140	125	265	154	137	291
15	Kongyong	400	374	774	456	426	882	664	540	1204	646	648	1294	717	719	1436	789	791	1580
16	Tal	175	151	326	200	172	372	290	218	508	283	261	544	314	290	604	345	319	664
17	Tange	304	273	577	347	311	658	505	394	898	491	473	964	545	525	1070	600	577	1177
18	Dumbi-Mungyim	194	175	369	221	200	421	322	252	574	313	303	616	348	336	684	383	370	753
19	Kongkhol/Others	254	252	506	290	287	577	422	364	785	410	436	847	456	484	940	501	533	1034
20	Yong/Others	474	401	875	540	457	998	787	579	1365	766	694	1460	850	771	1621	935	848	1783
21	Angwan Tungwut	55	80	135	63	91	154	91	115	207	89	139	227	99	154	252	109	169	278
	Total	4999	4923	9922	5699	5612	11311	8297	7103	15400	8078	8523	16601	8966	9461	18427	9863	10407	20270

Source: National population commission, 1991 population census of Nigeria.

References

Ames, C. G. (1934). *Gazetteers of Plateau Province*, Jos Native Authority, Vol. 4, p. 125.

Baklit, G. (1984). "The role of accessibility in rural marketing systems. A case study of Longkat Local Government Area in Plateau State, Nigeria." Unpublished B.A. thesis submitted to the Department of Geography, ABU, Zaria, Kaduna, and State, Nigeria.

Buchanan, K. M., and J. C. Pugh. (1971). *Land and People in Nigeria*, p. 11. London.

Colonial Records Hill Angas. Pankshin Division Reorganisation, file No. SNP 17/3/2156.

Colonial Records (1917). Chief of Pankshin and fifty-two others killed by Tal men. Ref. No. 1015/471p/1917.

Federal Office (1965). Population Census of Nigeria, Lagos.

Kowal, J. N., and D. T. Knobe. (1972). *An Agro-climatological Atlas of Northern State of Nigeria*, Zaria: ABU Press.

National Population Commission (1991). Final population result of Nigeria.

Temple, O. (1965). *Notes on the Tribes, Provinces, Emirates, and States of the Niger Delta*. London: Frank Cass and Co. Ltd., p. 8.

Chapter Two

Origin and Migration of Tal People

2.1 Tradition of Origin

Tal people in Plateau and Gombe States trace their origin to Yamel (Yemen) in the Middle East. Migratory movements brought them to Egypt, then to Ngazargamu in present-day Borno State. Although it is difficult to provide documented evidence of the nature of movements, dates, facts, and figures, oral tradition posits that they settled at the famous Tal Hill, known as "Lapang Tal" or "Pand Kilang" (present Shongom LGA in Gombe State). Movement to this site occurred after having passed through Koptu from Egypt, then to Tungo (Kaltungo LGA, Gombe State). According to ancestral evidence, the present location of Tal people in Gombe State is the seventh settlement after they left Yemen.

Movement is a dynamic process and definitely led to interaction with other people after departing from their place of origin. Regardless of the long period of separation, evidence of similarities can still be seen in the following areas:

a. The traditional method of installing and turbaning the chief of Tangale as an ethnic group, comprising Tanga Hung, Kalmai, Tal, Todi, Banganje, Tanglang, and Nate; this is similar to that of the Tal people in Pankshin Local Government Area in Plateau State. Both make use of locust bean tree leaves.
b. Use of hoes for the payment of dowry during the precolonial period, except for the difference in the size and shape of the hoes (large and small).
c. Agricultural practices and monthly calendars are tied to various activities during particular months of the year. Month in Tangale is known as "Tere" (Tal in Gombe) and is "Tai" (Tal in Plateau state).
d. Textile industry, arts, and crafts are the same.

The migration of Tal people to the present Kufai, Billiri LGA, is dated to the thirteenth century (Usman, 2006). It was while in Billiri that their identity became established and they started calling themselves "Tal."

According to oral traditions, Tal people trace their origin to Bornu, which they called "Bari" (Ames, 1934). Temple (1965) tends to confirm this view, saying that the people came from Korodofan, to Bornu, to Yam (see figure 2.1). Due to this link, they are regarded as "Abokin Wasa," playmates of the Beriberi and Kanuri. From Bornu, they left for Gugur in Amper (Kanke LGA) and then proceeded to Jepal (Mangu LGA). Their sojourn was short-lived as they continued from there to Tal Buzuk (Chip District), leaving behind some of their members at Jepal (Adamu Gutus Mutkhai, 1994). Again, they moved from Tal Buzuk to Damhi, then to Kwobzak, where they are today.

A more commonly shared view traces the origin of Tal people to the period when Angas people were driven from Kukawa in present Bornu State. When this happened, the Angas migrated to Dadin Kowa in Gombe State. While there, a misunderstanding among the people made one of the groups migrate to Billiri (Gombe State), and they settled at Tal (also in Gombe State). It was as a result of their settlement at Tal, the people started identifying themselves with the name Tal.

The Tal later continued their journey down to Zak (Wase LGA, Plateau State). After a while, they moved to Jivir and Kumbul (Kadung), a district in Pankshin LGA. From there they migrated to Jepal (Mangu LGA), where there was a division into three groups. The first group went to Kopal (Mangu LGA). The second group moved to Namu-jepjien (Qua'anpan LGA), while the third group, which maintained its identity as Tal, left Jepal for Latolong to Yentel-Damhi to Tadok-Kwopzak (all in present Tal District).

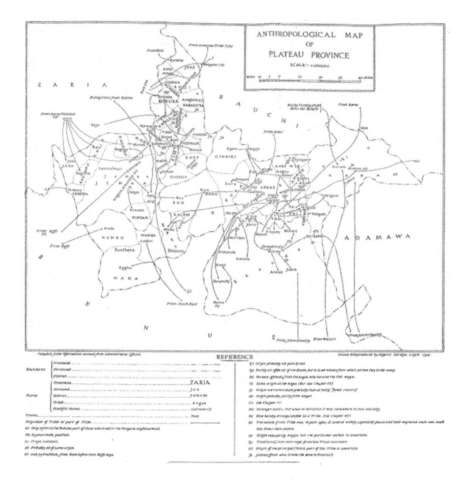

Figure 2.1: Anthropological map showing migration movements of Tal.

2.2 Tal Tradition of Origin in Relation to Chadic Speaking Group

It is evident from the account given that Tal people were originally part of the Angas people. Temple (1965) confirmed this position and referred to Tal as an Angas tribe. However, what is not fully known or confirmed is the time in history in which they separated and precisely when they arrived Tal, which was unoccupied.

A segment of Tal people who settled at Tadok witnessed a misunderstanding over leadership of idols in the shrine. The offending party was levied to pay a fine for its role in the squabble, but they objected and left in anger for Wullum in (Garram District in Kanke LGA), and later they went to Munok (Ampang District, Kanke LGA). By this time, they had multiplied in great numbers and had two families, called "Tori" and "Tokjen." The two families left Munok for Gugur (Amper, Kanke LGA), while some continued to Gazum (meaning "enter" in Tal language), where they split into three groups: Bwarat, Pilgani, and Zamko (all in Langtang North LGA, Plateau State).

2.3 Tradition of Origin in Relation to Those of Their Neighbours, Tarok and Goemai

According to oral tradition, through the Kwararafa linkage, Goemai, Chip, and Tal are from Wullum in Garram District, while Thel (Mikang LGA) are from Vongrong (Takong) in Tal District. As mentioned earlier, the Angas background gave birth not only to Tal but also to Taroh, who migrated from Tadok-Kwopzak in Tal. This forms the basis for the strong brotherhood that exists between Taroh and Tal, being from the same grandparents. This may also explain the similarities in names of the people and places of these two groups (e.g. Talbut and Talgwang). Even the origin of the ethnic name Taroh was Tallok (which means "Tal have increased"). "*Gazum*" means "enter" and "*Nankap*" means "God shares" in Tal. They share words like "*Na'an*" (the supreme being or God) and "*Ba*" ("come" in Tal). Other relationship aspects can be found in cultural and traditional activities, religious beliefs, and ways of worship. For example, Tal and Taroh have the same aspect of the performing arts, known as "*Komting*," which is a traditional dance concert by recognised, notable persons in traditional religion.

Traditional relationships in terms of origin also exist with Jepal, Kopal, Mernyang, Koenem, Doemak, Chip, and Namu People. They are also friendly with Pe (to the east), Piapung (to the south), and Garram (to the north) (Molynoux, 1917).

References

Ames, C. G. (1934). Chapter VI. Pankshin Division Gazetters of the Plateau Province, Nigeria, Volume IV, p. 147.

Ankruma, N. H. S. (2005). "Sources and prospects of Tangale history," in *Reconstructing African Past*. Gombe: Kumana Entreprises. pp. 63-135.

Colonial Record (1917). Sarkin Pankshin and thirty others killed by Tal men. Military patrols. File No. 10/5/47/p/1917.

Gabkwet, A. L. (2007). Informant interviewed on 04/03/2007 on the origin of Tal. Age 60 years.

Gupiya, Ambrose B. (2003). District head of Tal, interviewed on 08/03/2003 on history, tradition, and origin of the Tal people and their neighbours. Aged 65 years.

Mutkhai, Adamu Gutus (1994). First class chief, the Ngollong Ngas, of Pankshin LGA, interviewed on 04/04/1994 on the origin of Tal. Aged 75 years.

Pefwan, K. F. (2007). Informant interviewed on 04/04/2007 on the origin of the Tal people. Age 49 years.

Pembleton, E. S. (1940). Resident Plateau Province Records Tal District, Jos profile. File No. 1/1/3639. Tal District Pankshin Division1940-45.

Rumtong, B. M. (2007). Informant interviewed on 05/03/2007 on the origin of Tal. Age 53 years.

Tal Community Development Association (1988). Programme for Launching of N500, 000 Development Appeal Fund, at Nefur, Pankshin Local Government Area, Pankshin. pp. 10-11.

Temple, O. (1965). "Angas," in *Notes on the Tribes, Provinces, Emirates, and States of the Niger Delta*. London: Frank Cass Ltd., p. 8.

Tsetu, Rev. B. N. (2007). Informant interviewed on 05/03/2007 on the history and the origin of the Tal people. Age 57 years.

Tuna, J. G. (2007). Informant interviewed on 06/04/2007 on the history and the origin of the Tal people. Age 47 years.

Chapter Three

Precolonial Political Organisation

3.1 The Role of Chief-Priests (Clan Heads)

During the precolonial period, Tal people were divided into two distinctive political clan units: Zak and Yong. These clans did not have a common clan territory or centre. Members of the two clans were scattered and intermingled. The clan heads were called *Miskom Dil* (land leader). There were no rigid rules for succession and installation. They were selected and appointed based on merit and acceptability by the community. Thus, leadership was not hereditary (Dilkon, 1960).

Clan leaders were in charge of rituals of the people, while the *Gwolong Kum* was the head of the ancestral cult. Every clan had a specific centre (shrine) rather than a central place for performing rituals.

Zak had their shrines at Phyitei and Yong at Lazweng (Panglang). By tradition, the *Gwolong Kum* was chosen as a result of discussion between Kwopzak and Tangge at Paikhok. The people were then informed about the outcome. According to some informants, the *Gwolong Kum* was appointed by rotation (*Tungdeh*). He performed the following roles: if someone committed suicide by hanging on a tree, he was the one to cut the rope and dispose of the body, and he called people to adjudicate on disputes and settle conflicts (Dilkon, 1967).

Clan heads played different roles in Tal. For instance, it was believed that Zak brought dry season (*Luun*), while Yong was responsible for the rainy season. Zak was also concerned with *Nwong* (tutelary genius) (Meek, 1931). The choice of persons for leadership positions took cognisance of integrity, honesty, acceptability, knowledge of customs and traditions, wealth, and being free from criminal offences.

The chief of Kwopzak was the supreme religious authority for the entire Tal tribe. Each section had its own chief-priest, but all twenty-two villages recognised the chief of Kwopzak as their superior, and he performed the most important ceremonies, such as those connected with sowing.

The chiefs of Kadal, Koptaan, and Gyen were associated with the chief of Kwopzak in the performance of the more important rites and in matters affecting the tribe as a whole. The chief customarily consulted the heads of all sections. His position, therefore, was not one of pure autocracy. According to oral tradition, the compositions of the two clans were as follows:

(i) Zak clan consisted of Kwopzak, Kabiyak, Kyam, Takhong, Khalaap, Khongbong, Dimbyit, and Bakluwa (in Hamtul), Yentel and Damhi.

(ii) Yong was made up of the following areas: Tangge, Kabwai, Kajob, Dhan, Talkat, Hamtul, Basnuang, Zemsu, and Khongkol. However, there was no clear-cut separation between the two clans.

There were taboos surrounding chief-priests (clan heads). These include the following:

(i)   no contact with a woman under menstruation (*Mat gu kin khong*)
(ii)   no honey *titii* (*Mwai gu shang*)
(iii)   no *mes* (locust bean fruit)
(iv)   no *Ka'at* (a type of wild fruit)
(v)   no food with draw soup, such as *toklem* (*Karkashi* in Hausa) and *Dakyweng* (wild flowers of a particular type of tree)

Political and religious functions were not separated. For example, the clan heads were also in charge of political leadership as well as overseeing the religious activities of the land. Because of their prominent roles, they were expected to adhere strictly to the following rules:

(i)   They must not slap or hurt anybody in anger.
(ii)   They were not allowed to gossip.
(iii)   They should not befriend another man's wife.

15

Tal people had a unique way of handling political, religious, administrative, and judicial matters. Power was invested in the people who were in charge of a traditional institution called *"Paikhok"* located at Hamtul. The chief-priests (clan heads) were monitored under the umbrella of this institution, which was regarded as the National Assembly (Senate). Two persons, Kwaya and Tangge, presided over meetings from the beginning to the end.

The proceedings at Paikhok were as follows: Call for meeting was done by Kwaya and Tangge. The duo entered the shrine at the same time, and Kwaya would fire the first shot by calling Tangge by his nickname, *Kwalbang*, and would say, *"Nin-Sai hyi."* In response, Tangge, using Kwaya's nickname, would say, *"Dal lishyi,"* to confirm and acknowledge delivery of the message. Then discussion would ensue. However, before the sittings, Hamtul was always notified to make the necessary preparation of *duwaipeh* (ritual of putting protective medicine), but they did not talk during the monthly sittings at Paikhok. Meetings were always rounded up with prayers to God for a good harvest and prosperity.

At Paikhok, all matters, whether political, religious, or judicial, were discussed and decisions made, adopted, and implemented. The following rules were enacted at Paikhok:

Non-acceptance of guilt was resolved by taking on oath-swearing (*"Kum-suwa"*). This had great consequences for the guilty party; for example, loss of personal life or the entire family (generation). Principal offences, such as murder or involuntary confession of wizards, attracted capital punishment, or Na'an *tep*. This was considered as God's judgement.

Penalties varied according to the degree or nature of the offences. For instance, in a situation when a person hanged himself in front of another man's house (enemy) and the accused denied knowledge of the reason for causing this act of suicide, elders would ask him to swear an oath. If he was found guilty, he should pay *Kwet-kop Ni* (payment of fine to the idol and the deceased's uncles on his mother's side).

For other offences, such as wife beating or defiling a virgin, the fine of a cow was paid. The latter was regarded as the greatest sin to be committed in the community. Anyone who tampered with public natural resources, such as urinating, bathing, or passing excreta in drinking water, attracted severe punishment through *Mwandok tep*, which is capital punishment. Even adultery, sleeping with someone else's wife, attracted a fine of one cow. Also, it was a sacrilege to reveal the secrets of idols. Failure to inform in-laws or next of kin about the death of a wife, child, or son was a punishable offence. For criminal cases that attracted capital punishment, due processes were followed. A special sitting was made to establish the truth for final judgement. However, an extension of time was allowed for witnesses to be called from neighbours if necessary. A close relation, possibly a brother of his mother, was then called to present the culprit for execution. Passing a verdict of judgement was done by placing a green *khung* leaf (a type of wild plant) over the convict's head, signifying condemnation to death.

However, it is pertinent to note that judgement was done only by a person of wise counsel, good sense, and rational thought. Any wrong judgement could make the person lose his life or suffer mysterious sickness. Any strong disagreement concerning the judgement could be appealed at Paikhok but was subject to confirmation at Pangkhin.

The federal nature of Paikhok enforced equitable representation of Zak and Yong locality groups. No clan was superior to the other. The person chairing or presiding over meetings actually depended on where the matter was coming from. If from Zak, then Zak would preside, and vice versa. As mentioned earlier, Zak and Yong were intermingled and of equal status. But with time, Takhong or Vongrong (Zak) later assumed seniority because they had power as rain makers. So all cases of *gol pu'us* (lack of rain) were decided by Takhong.

Elected clan heads or leaders who attended meetings at Paikhok were expected to adhere strictly to a code of conduct, including the following:

(i)   to go almost naked by wearing only traditional triangular pant, *Thun gadi baba* in Tal (buttocks were exposed), *bente* (in Hausa)
(ii) not to be a gossiper
(iii) not to be a criminal or murderer
(iv) not to sleep with another man's wife
(v)   not to touch a corpse

17

(vi)   not to have contact with a woman under menstruation (they should not eat food cooked by her or share a dish)

During the precolonial period, the following traditional title-holders were in existence:

(i)   *Miskom Dil* (political administrative land leader)
(ii)   *Miskom Kum* (chief-priest)
(iii) *Miskom Lek* (warrior)
(iv)   *Miskom Yepkwet* (great leader of the wilderness and hunting)
(v)   *Gwolong Kum* (ancestral head and overall district head)

Titles were mostly hereditary or selected by appointment based on merit. However, in some instances, they were earned by initiation or bought (Dilkon, 1967).

Tal in Pankshin LGA, Plateau State, shares the same history of origin, values, and norms with Tal people in Gombe State. Traditionally, both groups

i.   exhibit due respect for elders, leaders, and constituted authority;
ii.   have high regard for due process in executing or carrying out activities or assignments for or on behalf of the people or communities as the case may be;
iii.   are God fearing, loving, friendly, and hospitable people;
iv.   exhibit maximum sincerity in their ways of life;
v.   uphold fundamental rights and freedom of expression;
vi.   believe in hard work to earn a living;
vii.   are naturally patriotic with a high sense of unity of purpose; and
viii. share the idea of a great ethnic brotherhood.

3.2 Council of Clans

3.2.1 Origin of *Nwong* in Tal

In one version of history, the clan council of Tal people had its origin through the marriage of an Angas woman from Kuwang (Ampang in Kanke LGA) to a man from Tangge (Tal, Pankshin LGA). By her first marriage at Kuwang, she gave birth to a son. But during a famine period, she came to Tal and remarried. This resulted in her giving birth to another son. The two sons grew up into adulthood independently, without having met or known each other. But they were told about each other's existence. The son at Tangge kept asking why his kith brother at Kuwang had never bothered to pay them a visit. He was told that one day during *Mwestai* his brother would come. It so happened that one day, his Kuwang brother came down to Tal. Beer (*mwes*) was brought, and the two brothers sat down and drank together. The mother asked whether they knew each other. They said no. At this point, they were told that they were brothers, the two sons she had been talking about. Full of surprise, they stood up, hugged each other, and said, "So you are the brother that my mother has been talking about." A bond of brotherhood and unity was established. After a few days, they both travelled back to Kuwang. Plentiful foodstuff was given to the Kuwang brother to take back home. The next day, they returned to Tal (Tangge) together. He spent a few days before going back. Again, he was given a lot of foodstuff to take home.

His visits became so frequent that his Tangge brother was disturbed. He asked him, "Why can't you come down and stay with us?" He pondered a while and said he had been given great responsibility at home, so he could not just abandon it. "What kind of responsibility is that?" his brother asked. He said he was holding *Nwong* and *Nen* (*Na'an* in Tal). His Tangge brother said he was interested in the god he brought. So the Kuwang brother agreed and an arrangement was made for them to meet at Langzok (in Tal) because he told him that *kum* would not be brought to the house. He came on the appointed day, but his Tangge brother did not turn up. He had left for Piapung (Mikang LGA) that morning on a drinking spree.

When the Kuwang brother got tired of waiting, he moved closer to Baden (in Kabwai) and waited in the shrine. He came out from his hiding place at several intervals to see whether his brother had shown up. Unknown to him, a woman from Kwaya, who was working on the farm with the men, had seen him. She told the men that this man had been waiting for so long and must be feeling hungry by now. Based on this report, he was given *youai* (gruel) to drink. The Kwaya man asked, "What is it that you have been waiting for so long?" He replied that he had an appointment with his kith brother at Tangge, that he had promised to bring something for him, but since he had not appeared, he would go back home. He told the Kwaya man that he brought *Nwong* (*Nen* or *Na'an*). The Kwaya man said he was interested. The Kuwang man said, "Since you were kind and gave me drink, there was no problem," so they went home together. As soon as he arrived in Kwaya, he immediately informed Koptaan that he had a visitor and that he should come so that they could keep what he brought in a shrine.

As a mark of appreciation, Kwaya brought a he-goat (*Daghung*) and Koptaan a castrated male goat (*ker hyi*) and gave it to the Kuwang man. He was pleased and appreciative of the kind gesture. He gave the Kwaya man a blessing and was empowered with the ability to find protective medicine and share it with Koptaan. Koptaan got nothing. Just when he had given his blessings, his Tangge brother arrived. His Kuwang brother was insulted and told him, "What kind of a stupid and useless person are you? You kept me waiting for so long; what if I was killed?" Having said that, he softened and controlled his temper, and told them that he was his brother. Now that he had given them what he brought, would they quarrel or be friendly and share it?

In response, they said why should they fight or quarrel over what was brought. This answer pleased the Kuwang man. He then told Kwaya that henceforth, he would be the person to find and provide medicine. Whatever happened, he had to inform Koptaan, who would in turn pass it to Tangge. This is the foundation of unity and origin of Nwong and council clans that meet periodically at Paikhok in Tal. Paikhok, located at Hamtul, was chosen because of its centrality. Membership during meetings came from Kwaya, Kopta'an, Tangge, and other local clan elders, recognised and qualified to attend.

3.2.2 The Second Version of the Origin of Nwong in Tal

According to oral tradition, Nwong originated from Garram in present Kanke LGA. This version is confirmed by elders and the chief of Tal, Ambrose B. Gupiya (JP). It was brought by one Dangvwai from Wullum in Garram during a visit to the home of *Dabang*, his ancestral parents at Kabwai. He informed his people that he came with *Nwong*, which plays a significant role in their livelihood. The story sounded so good, and they became interested and asked what it would cost for them to have it. In response, Dangvwai said it would only cost them a he-goat. Unfortunately, they did not have a he-goat, so he was taken to Kwaya. The importance of Nwong was explained but Kwaya was unable to produce a he-goat so that it could be established. After a fruitless attempt, Dangvwai advised Kwaya and Kabwai to take him to Gugyei at Kakikyang (*Pubum-kwopzak*). With proper briefing, Gugyei accepted it and brought a he-goat and gave it to Dangvwai as payment for the Nwong and performance of the rituals. However, Gugyei advised that it should be established at a central place. Hence, the siting of Ngat shrine at Kongnaan within Kwaya area (Dasuk).

Taking the lead as the first person to be initiated, Gugyei became the chief-priest while other interested persons were invited and initiated as *Dikum* (assistant chief-priests). These include Kabwai, Kwaya, Gosol, Kwali, Womnaan, and Fiyangshik. Other clans nearer to them were also introduced to *Nwong*. Those initiated as *Dikum* were usually recognised, creditable, and trusted men of substance.

The introduction of *Nwong* in Tal included

(i)   the rite of *Na'anshang,* also known as *Themghing*. This ritual marked the end of the circumcision ceremony;
(ii) burial ceremonies;
(iii) rite of harvest; and
(iv) rite of banning men and women from fighting, especially during the harvest period. In fact, all unnecessary quarrels were forbidden.

3.2.3 Warfare and Inter-Group Relations

Conscious of their survival, security issues were not left to chance. Each clan had a war chief (leader), but this depended very much on the side from where the war was coming. However, Ngwollong kum was recognised for the whole Tal. He was chosen on merit from a particular family. Tal people were prepared to defend their territory against external attack or invasion by intruders. Ritual elements were very important in warfare. As such, the *Gwollong Kum* performed the rituals in the *Lhiit* (shrine). The nature and form it took was very confidential, secret, and undisclosed. Warriors had to ensure that they took the relevant herbs and strictly observed taboos.

Tal people did not raid other groups for loot or slaves. Also, they did not suffer from raids by other groups.

However, they were engaged in formal warfare with the following groups:

1. Takhong fought with Thel (Montol), in Mikang LGA, over a land issue.
2. Takhong fought with Piapung (south) over a boundary demarcation dispute (*Yit Kakwui dil*).
3. Takhong fought with Angas (in the north) over a boundary dispute at Kabang between Ranme and Deshi (who incidentally were friends).

A warrior who took a human head was regarded as a hero by the community. There were also rituals surrounding the making of a hero. The most important was through *Vwang* (an initiation ceremony) to protect him from the blood of the slain enemy. Heroes were decorated with red and black feathers. Such a person became leader of war (*Gwollong lek*). Also a person who killed a wild animal, such as a leopard (*khung*), lion (*lit*), or buffalo (*khiin*), was declared a hero. The skin of the animal was usually wrapped in *kommes* (locust bean leaves) and hung on his door.

Heroes enjoyed privileges such as being given preferential treatment at ceremonies or festivities during their lifetime. Upon their demise, they were given a heroic and befitting burial. For example, the head of the slain enemy was brought out for the *poll* (funeral ceremony). People would weep, show deep emotional feelings, and cry openly, expressing deep regrets over the demise of an important personality.

Tal people are known for being friendly and socially outgoing. They maintain cordial relationships with their immediate neighbours. This is largely responsible for the few cases of inter-tribal wars and absence of political hostility. There were no festivities in existence for them to attend and partake among their neighbours. There was trade by barter exchanges. Intermarriages were very rare except with the Angas because of their common place of origin. Tal is not a closed society, because there are tendencies of cultural exchange, like *Nwong* and *Tau*, which they took from the Angas people. Also, they borrowed *Khiyim* from Thel, Fwa'an from Goemai, and *Kakuu* (cornstalk flute, for cultural dances) from the Chip and Mernyang people.

3.3 Tal People and Other Tribes within Zaria Province during the Precolonial Era: The Practice of Head-Hunting and Cannibalism

The people of Tal were just like other ethnic groups that existed during the dark era. Human beings have fallen short of the glory of God, according to the Christian scriptures. This means that there is no perfect ethnic group.

Societal expectations for good human behaviour is quite high. However, it is unfortunate that people took part in unimaginable rituals, like head-hunting and cannibalism. Involvement in these practices, according to some informants, was to show prowess, and they believed that the taste of the enemy's blood led to self-empowerment, confidence building, and energy, and it helped them maintain an intimidating posture. This was the general practice; it is on record that many tribes located in the central pagan belt, extending from Yola to the confines of Zaria province, practiced head-hunting and cannibalism during the precolonial era. The following is a list of the head-hunting tribes:

Munshi	Jera	Jukun	Kagoma
Ankwe	Wurkum	Kibalo	Bolewa
Owe	Teria	Anaguta	Kinuku
Kagoro	Katab	Bachama	Irigwe
Basange	Ataka	Bata	Idoma
Kaje	Berom	Okpoto	Igbira
Hill	Mada	Tera	Kitimi

The following were admittedly cannibalistic:

Tangale	Montoil	Waja
Kamu	Tula	Longuda
Angas	Yergam	Chum
Rukuba	Sura	Warjawa
Ganawuri	Jarawa	Zumper
Piri	Tal	Nungu
Plain Mada	Pe	Borok
Hill Angas (plain Angas deny)	Mama	Kushi
Jengre	Pero	Iyashi
Gusum	Bangunji	Kaleri
Ngel	Ninzam	Chawai
Awok	Mufon	

(Source: Meek, 1931)

The long list for either head-hunting or cannibalism shows that many ethnic groups were guilty of having committed serious crimes against humanity in the past. However, Temple (1965) said that cannibalism was abandoned at the time of British occupation.

References

Ames, C. G. (1934). *Gazetteer of Northern Provinces of Nigeria: The Highland Chieftances.* Vol. IV, p. 125.

An ethnographic account of the northern provinces of Nigeria together with the report on the 1921 Deccinial census (p. 12).

Dilkon, W. W. (1967). "An outline of Tal history." Unpublished document.

Gukyem, Anthony T. (2003). An informant interviewed on Tal's origin and precolonial organisation. Interviewed on 08/03/2003. Age 57 years.

Gupiya, Ambrose B. (2003). The district head of Tal interviewed on precolonial organisation. Interviewed on 26/01/2003. Age 65 years.

Gutong, Kumwuaih G. (2003). Interviewed on 08/03/2003 on the origin and precolonial organisation of Tal. Age 65 years.

Guyit, Mwangyes (2003). Ward head of Kabwai. Interviewed on 16/08/2004 on the origin and precolonial organisation of Tal. Age 80 years.

Lafot, Mutshel (2003). Interviewed on 10/03/2003 on the origin and precolonial organisation of Tal. Age 58 years.

Meek, C. K. (1931). *The Northern Tribes of Nigeria*. Volume II. London: Frank Cass and Co. Ltd., pp. 48-49.

Rumtong, Mitok Yakubu (2003). Informant interviewed on 16/12/2003 on the history of Tal. Age 90-plus.

Temple, O. (1965). "Angas," in *Notes on the Tribes, Provinces, Emirates, and States of the Niger Delta*. London: Frank Cass and Co. Ltd.

Usman, J. (2006). *A Concise History of Tal in Tangale Maidom*. Gombe Nigeria.

Chapter Four

Precolonial Economy and Social Organisation

4.1 Precolonial Economy: An Overview

Before the coming of colonial masters, agriculture was the mainstay of the economy. Farming was the major economic activity of the people of Tal. As farmers, they cultivated crops as well as kept livestock. The economy was underdeveloped based on primary production, and subsistence farming was the major type of agricultural practice. Most of the farmers cultivated and produced crops such as groundnuts (*khomdut*), guinea corn (*swa'ah*), millet (*maiah*), bambra nuts (*khom*), cowpeas (*ihyim*), digiteria varities (*duala* and *duala shit*), tobacco (*tabba*), pumpkins (*biyap*), yam (*bhem*), sweet potatoes (*khunkhung*), pepper (*shita'am*), cotton, (*fieu*) and cocoyam (*gwan*). Other crops grown were okro (*tokla*), beniseed (*lem*), *Sai,* and *saikwan* (all varieties of melon crops, close to *egusi*, oily in nature).

Apart from crop cultivation, they planted tree crops of economic value such as olive trees, *canarium sweinfurtii* (*Ting Pa'at /Itili,* in Hausa), mahogany (*Ting Kho-ok*), desert palm (*borasus*), locust bean (*Ting Mes*), baobab (*Ting-Tonin*), mango (*Ting Mangoro*), silk cotton (*khiyi*), and oil palm (*Mwaibhang*). These trees had great economic value. For instance, *Itili* and mahogany were sources of precious medicinal oils. The gum from *Itili* was used to drive snakes out of the house, while that of *thyiem* (a tree bigger than mahogany) was burned for light. Desert palm (*borasus*) fruits (see plate 4.2) were eaten and the seeds were buried in the ground. After one year, they were removed, cooked and eaten as *laigang* (*muruchi* in Hausa). The tree itself is a major source of timber for roofing houses even to the present.

Figure 4.1: Silk cotton tree. One of the major economic trees that attracted Hausa traders to settle at Balong-Tal, headquarters of the district during colonial rule (1914).

Figure 4.2: Desert palm (*borasus*) (*Ting Gang* in Tal). The fruits are edible; when placed in the ground it will germinate like carrot. After a year, it can be harvested, cooked, roasted, and eaten or sold. It has medicinal value

especially when eaten raw. It is a source of timber for roofing, and the leaves are used for making local mats (*Karangang*). It is also a source of fuel wood.

Crop cultivation was done alongside with animal husbandry and livestock keeping. Animals such as sheep (*Thim*), goats (*ihyi*), and cattle (*Muturu, Ning Tal*) were reared. Free ranching was adopted in most instances for keeping the animals. Almost all households kept poultry (*khe*) or ducks (*Gwa-gwa*) for various purposes.

Formal markets were not in existence, so most of the trade and exchange of good and services were done by barter. There were also other economic activities such as local textile industry producing *Thel*, *Tuun*, cap weaving, wood or calabash carving, poetry, blacksmithing, hunting, and local beer brewing (*mwes* or *burkutu* in Hausa).

4.2 Calendar of Tal

Activities of the people of Tal were done according to the calendar of the year. The months of the year in Tal are as follows:

1.   Gyong lu'un January
2.   Fiya Yang Fiya Khiihyi February
3.   Tong Lu'un turdhung March
4.   Barang April
5.   Ninfwen May
6.   Tongyouai June
7.   Maihpiya July
8.   Nwong August
9.   Dong September
10. Taikhung October
11. Datutwaih November
12. Du'un December

Every month has a unique name. An interesting aspect of the naming of the months is the fact that they are activity oriented. For instance, *Tongyouai* (June) indicated when people kept watch over their crops and drove birds away from destroying crops, especially millet. This naming pattern was a clear indication that the Tal people were agriculturalists.

4.3 Land Tenure

When the people came to Tal, the land was unoccupied, virgin, and highly forested. This meant that ownership and occupation of any given land or farm depended very much on the principle of "first come, first served." This included the permission of an individual or group to cut down trees or clear and acquire any land size. This was how they originally occupied and claimed ownership of the land. A father could give some portion of his farm to his grown children (males). However, the children could also find their own pieces of land to farm or occupy.

Land could be obtained or acquired through any of the following ways:

(i) **Borrowing or loan:** This happened when a man asked a friend or relative to give him a piece of land to farm. The period was specified, for example, a year.

(ii) **Sale or mortgage:** A person who had a large expanse of land and lacked the capacity to farm it all had the right to sell or mortgage part of it to anyone who was in need. Elders, relatives, or neighbours were invited to witness the transaction. This was to forestall any conflict or disagreement in future over how it all happened. However, the land or farm could be redeemed if the owner wanted his property back. A refund of what was paid (for instance, if it was two or three baskets of beans or groundnuts) would be required. With evidence of payment verified, the land was retrieved.

(iii) **Clan land:** Land ownership in Tal was collective. Individuals had only usufrunct rights (rights of enjoyment). No single member of the family could lay claim over the land. Any or all members either farmed together or shared portions to work on.

(iv) **Inheritance:** This was a situation where a father had grown children and gave them portions of his land to farm. When their own children grew to adulthood, the land would become theirs, and their own children could also inherit it.

(v) **Extended family kind:** Land could be obtained through extended family linkage by marriage from the mother's or father's side. This was a traditionally recognised method of sustaining unity, family ties, and friendship practised from the past to the present. For instance, land could be obtained from the mother's kindred (*kinmwa*) or uncle (*kawu* in Hausa).

4.3 Farming Systems

Tal people did not practice sudden farming (that is, a system where the entire settlement moved away from an area due to decline in soil fertility). But they did practice "slash and burn" (bush fallowing) type of farming. This was done when they noticed that the soil had become impoverished due to continuous farming over the years. The farm was allowed to lie fallow for a few years so that the natural process of soil regeneration could take place. After the soil became fertile again, they could resume farming.

There were two types of farmlands: *Mai yep* (bush farm) and *Daful* or *mai phyipang* (compound farm). A bush farm was sometimes smaller in size than a compound farm. Farm sizes ranged from one to five hectares. The principal crops grown included groundnuts (*khomdut*), guinea corn (*swa'ah*), and bambra nut (*kom*). Men, women, and children worked on the farms. During farming, men prepared the ridges (cross banding) while the women and children did the sowing or planting of the seeds. Harvesting of guinea corn was done mainly by men, but strong women also participated. For groundnuts and bambra nuts, men, women, and children were actively involved.

A compound farm was the main farm and was larger in size. Inter cropping or mixed farming was practiced on this farm. The principal crops grown included *maaihyi* (millet), *swa'ah* (guinea corn), *ihyim* (beans or cow peas), *Duala* and *Duala shit* (varieties of digitera), *khutung* (*tamba* in Hausa), *bhem* (yam), *gwan* (cocoyam), and *quewang* (finger millet, *dauro* in Hausa). Other crops grown were *biyap* (pumpkins), *tokla* (okra), *shitaam* (pepper), *lem* (beniseed), *nwes* (African curry), *khungkhung* (sweet potatoes), *sai* and *sai kwan* (traditional melon varieties).

4.3.1 Land Management

Tal people tilled or cultivated the land before planting their crops. Over the years, they practised cross banding or box type of ridge making (see figure 4.3). This insured retention of soil fertility and sustainable crop production. Terracing was also practiced to check erosion and maintain the nutrient content of the soil to ensure bountiful crop yield from the farms.

Figure 4.3: Agricultural ridge making or cross banding of the Tal people (*Maitilli*). This soil-conservation technique checkmates soil erosion and maintains fertility of the soil. It has been practiced since colonial times.

Crops grown together were guinea corn, millet, and beans, and also millet and groundnuts. It was believed that beans and groundnuts were nitrogen-fixing crops with the potential to enhance soil fertility. Hence, they promoted growth and high yield of crops. Guinea corn and groundnuts were rarely inter-cropped. This was because of the height of guinea corn, which could over-shadow the groundnut crops, thereby affecting photosynthesis (growth process). When this happened, certainly groundnuts would not do well under such conditions.

The farm was worked by men, women, and children. *Khen* (land clearing) and *fwui* (weeding) were done by all, as was pruning of guinea corn leaves. Harvesting millet and guinea corn was done mainly by men, though sometimes women also participated. Thus, it was possible to identify division of farm work in Tal according to gender (see table 3.1).

Table 4.1: Farming Labour by Gender

S/No	Type of Farming Activity	Gender	Crop Type and Month
1.	Terracing, using stones and corn stalks (*yanglet*)	Women	Any crop, March-April
2.	Land clearing (*khen*)	Women and children	March-April
3.	Sowing/planting (*khop*)	Men, women, and children	April-May, millet and guinea corn
4.	*Bubuk* (earthing up)	Men, women, and children	June-Principal crops: guinea corn and millet
5.	*Fwui* (first weeding)	All	May, millet and guinea corn
6.	Harvesting	Mainly men and women collect	July-August, millet, November-December, guinea corn
7.	Threshing, winnowing	Women	All season

Source: Field work, 1998, 2003/2004.

Table 4.1 indicates division of labour in farming activity by gender among the Tal people. For instance, *khen* (land clearing), winnowing, and threshing were done by women, while the men did most of the harvesting work. Making terracing with corn stalks (*yanglet*) was only done by women.

4.4 Unit of Labour and Cooperative Approaches to Farming

The basic unit of farm labour was the nuclear family. That is, the man, his wife or wives, and children. If any family relation was living with him, they also assisted on the farm. Outside the family setting, Tal people had three basic cooperative methods of mobilising people for farm labour. These were (i) *Mai mwes* (mobilising people by brewing local beer), (ii) *Khielmwan* or *zellet,* and (iii) *Gaya* (*Maiphim* in Tal).

(i)   **Mai mwes** was organised by persons (male or female) who had large expanses of farmland and needed extra hands to cultivate all the land. They could brew local beer and invite able-bodied people to come and work for them on their farmlands. As they worked, *tulet* (breakfast beer) was served during break time, 9-10 a.m. Later, towards afternoon, *dha puss* was from 1 to 2 p.m. and finally in the evening between 4 and 5 p.m. At closing hour, *mwes mai* was given in about seven calabashes (*lalit*) to every participant.

(ii)   **Khielmwan/zellet** was when a father who had children of marriageable age (boys or girls) brewed local beer and invited their friends to come and work on his farm. But *namang* was when a suitor of a girl organised his friends to go and work on his father-in-law's farm once a year.

(iii)   **Maiphim** was rotational farming (*tungdhe*) among groups of people in the locality, organised according to an arrangement in a socially acceptable manner. At times, it could be by age groups.

4.5 Rituals Attached to Farming

Before farming commenced, *Na'an* must be worshipped at Paikhok. The *Gwolong Kum* (chief-priest) would start. After the elders have met, the following rituals were performed.

(i)   **Planting (*khop*).** Following the meeting and prayer at Paikhok, members collected medicine for distribution to their people, who would put it on their farms. This was done by symbolic representation such as placing fresh leaves (*khom wu'ut*) or *Caricapapaya* (*gwandan' daji* in Hausa) tied to a stick and fixed at strategic edges of farmlands. The purpose was to prevent *gup* or *mai gu mang*: taking away the farm blessing of good yield and bountiful harvest.

(ii) **Harvesting millet (*Maaih gu dhip*) in August.** The process was the same as in planting but here, the people were given knives for the harvest of millet by the chief-priest. It is the same for guinea corn when they received a knife (*kik*). *Nwong paaiyhi suwa* (idol of guinea corn) drove away all bad evils that would destroy the blessings of good harvest by the end of November.

(iii) ***Mwa phistai.*** At the full moon, mid-October was a time of freedom and peace when people blew horns or whistles, danced, and organised festivals; it also marked the end of marriage season. This was an event during which a spear was used to shoot at the base of the ripe guinea corn crop. Men used it to show off, to demonstrate having attained man-hood, to symbolise their bravery, or as proof of being real men, ready for action. When this was done, it marked the time to commence harvesting guinea corn.

It must be noted that the *Gwolong Kum* was always the first to start anything pertaining to farm activity before other people, after having met at Paikhok. The farming calendar was derived through this traditional institution (see table 4.2).

Table 4.2: Paikhok Farming Calendar (Tal)

S/No	Type of Farm Activity (Major)	Month	Crop Type/Secondary Activity
1.	*Khen* (land clearing)	March-April	*Yanglet* (Terracing, using corn stalks)
2.	*Khop* (planting/sowing)	April-May	Guinea corn and millet
3.	*Fwui* (weeding)	May	Guinea corn and millet
4.	*Bubuk* (earthing up)	June	Sowing groundnuts and bambra nuts
5.	*Maaiyhi le vu'ut* (millet ripening sign)	June-July	Sowing cowpeas
6.	*Khik* (harvest)	July-August	Harvesting millet, planting sweet potatoes

S/No	Type of Farm Activity (Major)	Month	Crop Type/Secondary Activity
7.	*Swah le vuut* (guinea corn ripening sign)	September-October	Pruning of guinea corn leaves, making ridges to support guinea corn and beans
8.	*Dhyip* (harvest of guinea corn)	November-December	Harvesting: bambra nuts, guinea corn, and sweet potatoes
9.	*Khik Nphap* (end of harvest period)	December-February	(Rest period)

Source: Fieldwork, 2003

The information in table 4.2 shows a calendar of farming of Tal people in phases according to the months of the year. All the activities, listed by tradition, can only be done after a meeting was held at Paikhok.

4.6 Animal Husbandry and Livestock

Tal people kept livestock as well as practiced agriculture. The following types of animals were reared:

(i)   *Ihyi* (goat)
(ii) *Thim* (sheep)
(iii) *Ningtal* (cow, shorthorn; *muturu* in Hausa)
(iv) *Khe kin gwagwa* (poultry, local chickens and ducks)
(v)   *Bishing* (horses obtained from Angas)
(vi) *Ass* (dog)

Animal husbandry and livestock keeping had great significance in the lives of the Tal for the following reasons:

1. They made use of the waste as organic fertiliser (*fhip*). For the growth of crops like millet, goat waste was applied.
2. Payment of *kwetkah* (a fine paid to bail themselves out when they had committed an offence).

35

3.   *Ninmut* (announcement/notification of death and funeral ceremony). First, a female goat was given to the first cousin or uncle on the mother's side to inform them about the death. This was done by adult males only. As soon as a male died, a senior person from the family of the deceased, by tradition, must produce a live animal to be given to the relations and also to be used for preparing food (*gwom piya*) for all those who had come to mourn the dead. Lastly, after the morning period, *kwet kop* (another goat) was given to the relatives.

4.7   Payment of Dowry

Bride price or dowry was paid using a cow, goat, or sheep. For instance, for a young man to get married, his parents must produce a cow, or ten goats, or twelve sheep. If a man could not pay, he would remain a bachelor. However, this could be redeemed. His uncles or kinsmen could rally round themselves to produce what was required to get a wife for their son.

4.8   Hunting

Hunting was a very prestigious activity, although agriculture produced more food. This was so because it provided an opportunity for people to show that they were real men of bravery and strength. It was a recreational activity, especially during the dry season.

Hunting was also done for happiness, especially when someone killed one of the most highly valued or appreciated wild animals such as buffalo (*khin*), elephant (*knee*), lion (*lhit*), or leopard (*khung*). It would be used for *mab* or *pwol* during his funeral ceremony. Hunting would also drive away wild animals and keep them from destroying farm crops.

There were two types of hunting in Tal. These were (i) individual and (ii) group.

(i)   **Individual.** There were no professional hunters in Tal. It was a part-time practice. Hunting was a dry season activity. Only a few men, like *Mangkhung*, hunted throughout the year.

(ii) **Group hunting**, known as *yeplu*, was organised to mark the death of an elderly man who died before March or April. It was a kind of thanksgiving when the uncles on the mother's side were finally paid the inheritance due to them. This was done regardless of religious belief. However, *yeplu* was mainly for traditional practice. If any game was killed, the hand must be given to the house of the deceased.

Communal or group hunts, in which all adult males in a particular locality participated, were:

(i) *Gabdong* (ii) *Pa'al Na'an* (iii) *Gumtushuwep* (iv) *Sanpaal* (v) *Dunglut-Kwopzak* (vi) *Fungpang* (vii) *Kapa'ai* (big one), (viii) *Kagong*, (ix) *Kopfyei* (*Basnuwang*), and (x) *Khatog* (*Basnuang*). Others were *Dong Ningkam, Don Sweigwim, Pang Nadu* (Chip District), *Pang Longmar* (Chip District), *Tonshing, Yep Khaki, Langdha, Wankhai, Dumkinyit, Gabdawa, Nalik,* and *Konglewer,* organised by Dungyel and Tihl people in Garram District. Thus, hunting did not take place in the same place or area every year. Locations were changed and neighbouring groups to these hunts were invited in turns. It is difficult to provide dates for these hunts because of the absence of writing in the culture; records were not kept.

Hunting techniques employed during communal hunts involved using tactical movements from strategic positions. Those with dogs were in front, followed by people with bows and arrows at the rear. The group movement was done according to clans and locality.

The reasoning behind the formation was that if somebody shot a wild animal, his people would quickly join hands so that he did not get killed. It also served as a guard against disputes, seizures, and fights over an animal of high value like *khung* (leopard) or *pahap* (antelope).

Sharing of the game was done according to clans. Communal hunts usually brought disputes and fights, especially when one clan claimed another clan's game by force. This caused bad feelings with neighbouring groups, but it was usually quickly resolved. The intervention of *Gwollong Tal* was used as a last resort. After judgement, payment of a fine was made. Then the matter was put to rest, and the parties concerned would forgive and forget.

It is pertinent to note that the person who fixed the hunt had to be very clean; he did not sleep with his wife or any other woman. In addition to hunting animals, there were people who would go to collect honey from the bush for consumption or to use as a gift, but not for exchange or sale. This was mainly done by hunters who were very familiar with the bush, but later on the youth and women joined them.

4.9 Economic Trees and Forest Products

Tal has many valuable trees and forest products (see table 4.3):

Table 4.3: Economic trees, forest products, and their values

S/NO	Name/Specie	Value and Use
1.	Locust beans (*Tingmes*)	Firewood, preparation of local Maggie (*tidhip, Dadawa* in Hausa) Surgery, plastering, and poison for dressing arrow heads/ catching fish
2.	Mango (*Mangoro*) mangifera indica.	Fruits, medicine, and firewood
3.	Desert palm (*Borasus*) Ting gang)	Timber, fruits, leaves for mat making, edible roots (*lai gang*), bed, local cushion for sitting or lying down, rain coat, and bag making.
4.	Palm tree, palm oil (*Ting mwaibang*)	Oil, fruits, brooms from the leaves
5.	Tamarind (Tamarindus indica, *Dhyis*)	Fruits and wood, gruel making, and medicine (diuretic)
6.	Silk cotton (*Ting khyihi, Rimi* in Hausa)	Wool for making mattresses, pillows, and fruits, making soup with products of the seeds (called "*gai*"), local varieties of Maggie

S/NO	Name/Specie	Value and Use
7.	Boabab, classified as Adansonia digitata (*Ting Tonin, Kuka* in Hausa)	Fruit, vegetable soup, cloth and rope making, local Maggie, and arrow-proof vest
8.	Olive tree (*Itili,* camerium in Hausa) (*Tingpa'at*)	Oil, gum used for medicine
9.	Moringa (*Zhogali* in Hausa, *Ting shangham*)	Vegetable soup and medicine
10.	Sheabutter (*Ting dhyin*)	Fruits, oil, medicine, and firewood
11.	*Kanya* (*Ting Yubi*)	Fruits, twigs used as local tooth brush paste, medicine, and firewood
12.	*Kurna* (Hausa), (*Gyelhit* in Tal)	Fruits, bow, fence, wood
13.	*Kyemdwhang*	Fruit, wood
14.	Blackberry (*Malmo,* n Hausa, *Feeh* in Tal)	Fruit, wood
15.	*Adua, Eikhung*	Fruits, wood, medicine
16.	Fig tree (*Tuwas*)	Leaves, fodder, fruits, and medicine
17.	*Gunglong*	Medicine and leaves used for making local meat pie (*Nguk*); sap is used for poison arrow heads
18.	*Khe'en*	Medicine, fruits, and wood
19.	*Gwalzhak*	Fruits/wood
20.	*Caripapaya, Whu'ut* (*Gwandandaji* in Hausa)	Fruits, medicine (iodine), religious practice
21.	*Chiwo* (Hausa), *Kha'at*	Fruits, wood, and rope making
22.	Fruit (*Ghei*)	Fruit, fence, and wood
23.	*Gwogwo* (in Tal)	Fruit, medicine
24	*Bwongpit*	Fruit, medicine

S/NO	Name/Specie	Value and Use
25.	*Dinya* (in Hausa) *Dhep* (in Tal)	Firewood, fruits, leaves used for soup making and medicine
26.	*Bongbong*	Fruits and wood
27.	Mahogany (*khok*)	Oil/wood, medicine, and timber-door/bed making
28.	*Thiehm*	Timber and gum, used as local candle for lighting
29.	*Rham*	Fruits, wood

Different people in the community valued trees for many reasons. For instance, they were valued particularly by woodcarvers, house builders, and charcoal burners. Mahogany was used by woodcarvers; builders preferred *borasus* for roofing; and charcoal burners used *Ra'an* and *Kha'aphan* trees.

Oil was extracted from *itili canrium sweinfurthi*, Bush candle (*paat*), using the following process:

(i)   Pluck the fruit. When ripe, they are ebony in colour.
(ii)   Use lukewarm water (not boiling) and put the fruits inside the pot for about ten minutes.
(iii) When it is done, it becomes soft. Drain the water, put it inside mortar, and pound it.
(iv)   After pounding, add a small amount of water and return to fire. As it boils, the oil will float on top, so you can then extract the oil by steaming.

Some trees such as locust bean (*ting mes*) produced fruits that were used for making highly protein-rich, local traditional Maggie called *tidip*. The process of producing it is as follows:

(i)   Pluck the ripe fruits (golden yellow) and allow them to dry.
(ii)   Take off the soft part, separate the seeds, and dry.
(iii) Cook the seeds for a few hours until the hard black cover is soft and can be removed or washed easily.
(iv)   After washing, cook it again for about an hour.

(v)   Remove from the fire, drain the water, and place in one or two baskets (depending on the quantity). Cover with mango leaves or *gunglong* (species of fig tree) and allow to ferment by keeping in a warm place for three days.

(vi) Remove the leaves, allow it to dry a little, pound it, and then mould it into desired shape or size into *tidhip* (*dadawa* in Hausa).

Economic trees such as locust bean, palm oil, olive, silk cotton, mango, and desert palm (*borasus*) were deliberately planted. However, those found on the farm when it was acquired by the landowner were preserved. In some instances, economic trees could be inherited separately from the land, but in other instances, they went together. Thus, if the land belonged to you and trees were planted, the ownership was yours. But if the land was not yours and you wanted to plant economic trees, permission must be obtained from the landowner before planting was done. If the land and the tree belonged to you, you would inherit both. But if the land did not belong to you and you planted economic trees, then you may inherit only the trees.

Women did not go into the bush to collect the fruits of certain trees. Men and shepherd boys or male youth went and brought fruits like *feeh* (*Malmo* in Hausa), *yubi, gyelhit* (*kurna*), *gwalzhak gwogwo, ghei, wuut* (*gwandan daji* in Hausa), *bongbong, rhaam, khen, hheng,* and root plants like *bhest.* By tradition, it was the responsibility of the women of the household to collect firewood (*shieep*) for domestic use.

4.10 Methods of Storage

To avoid possible losses of farm crops, different methods of storage were adopted. For effective preservation, crops were allowed to dry very well before storage. For instance, guinea corn and millet were harvested and dried properly in the open sun. In fact, during the drying process of millet, quarrels often developed if the wife, husband, or children allowed rain to beat it.

They applied pounded herbs with medicinal value or local potash (*shiem*) or ash (*fwet*) on any given crop to be preserved for storage. If the crop was wet, it was allowed to dry for three to four days.

Traditional methods of storing millet and guinea corn were granary (see Figure 4.4, *Mhe*), *kha pai* or *gazhii* for millet (figures 4.5 and 4.6). Fire was often burned in a makeshift kitchen under the granary. This also helped in preservation and storage. But for other crops like digitaria or groundnut, they could be kept in a giant pot (*palang*) or granary. They usually separated the good (high quality) and low-graded crops before preservation and storage. The low-graded one was consumed first.

Figure 4.4: *Mhe*: Granary for storing grains such as millet and guinea corn

Figure 4.5: Traditional method of storing millet and sorghum

Figure 4.6: Traditional method of storing millet and guinea corn

4.10   Insects and Other Pests

A large swarm of locusts (*Quel*) attacked the community three times during the precolonial period. Other insects such as big ants (*tithing*), termites (*khyeiyeng jha*), and white ants (*jhieu*) often attacked crops in the community, but not on a large scale as it was with the locust.

4.11 Traditional Crafts

4.11.1 Iron Smelting: Tal people practised iron smelting. The raw material called *girib* was available at Takhong, Gyeri, and Dong Semun (Kwopzak). People with a special ability ("third eye") surveyed, identified, located, and searched for the iron ore. They were called "*kangkha gu manbi*" and believed to possess supernatural powers, which enabled them to locate possible sites of the iron ore. They were expected to observe some taboos like no sexual intercourse, avoiding contact with women under menstruation, and no eating of locust bean fruit or draw soup (*toklem*).

The type of furnace used was a very simple one. The ground was dug and logs of wood (wet and dry) were burnt over the place, thus firing with a special type of firewood (*ran, kass,* and special trees obtained from the forest). Between ten and fifteen people were involved in smelting the iron ore. There was no master smelter. The process took one to three weeks, after which iron was obtained. It looked like small stones, black like coal but solid. A kind of special clay called *mwalak* was used to mix with *girib* to produce the iron. The finished product was a small piece of irregularly shaped iron.

As a reward, those involved in iron smelting were given part of the end product. The finished products, small pieces of iron, were used for domestic purposes. That is, for the production of hoes of different shapes and sizes, arrows, or bangles. In some instances, it was exchanged in trade by barter for goats, chickens, or cows, depending on the size.

4.11.2 Blacksmithing: There were blacksmiths in precolonial Tal society. They were highly respected and regarded as chiefs in their own rights because it was also believed that they possessed supernatural powers. As a taboo, the blacksmithing house was out of bounds to women observing menstruation periods. In terms of number, about five were practising. But with time, the number increased as other people with interest learned from the first tradesmen.

Bellows were *khulluks* made from animal skins, which were used to blow the fire to keep it glowing. Two or three people were required for this process. In most cases, only one person in addition to the blacksmith was needed. Persons wanting tools made for them did not bring their own iron; it was provided by the blacksmiths. Payment to the blacksmiths was negotiable. One might pay with *sai thun* (a woven clothing material), a goat, a chicken, or even by working on the blacksmith's farm.

Blacksmiths made many items. These include *kop* (spear), *khyan* (hoe), *pas* (arrow), *dirrh* (arm bangle), *eihghyt* (see figure 4.7, used on the leg for special dances), *khik* (knife), *gye-ep* (sickle), *sep* (axe), *ngan* (ring), *kassban* (wrist bangle), *gwangsang* (a kind of circular iron put on hunting stick, *baal shaal*), farming hoe, and *khyan long* (very large hoe used mainly for payment of dowry). The work of a blacksmith was combined with farming. It was not seasonal but was a year-round activity.

Figure 4.7: Eihghyt: Worn on the ankle and used for special cultural dances.

4.11.3 Pot Making: In Tal, the principal potters were women found in the following localities:

(i) Tangge (*Natong*)
(ii) Kongkhol (*Natong Ghitle*)
(iii) Kabyak (*Vhem Vhem*)
(iv) Mudong (*Maidil*)
(v) Kabwai (*Ningyet*)
(vi) Kwopzak
(vii) Kyam (*Talvyak*)
(ix) Mungne
(x) Khong balaam
(xi) Tunbik Gaplhiit

In addition to the names listed above, there were experts in many other locations in Tal. Clay was readily available in Tal, but some women from Tangge and Mudong, among other places, used to travel to Kongkhol to obtain it.

The process by which pots were made was as follows:

(i) Dig and obtain the clay and allow it to dry properly.
(ii) Pound some of the clay to powder (dry) and soak the remaining clay.
(iii) Mix the soaked and powdered clay. Then mould, by coiling to desired shape and size. It took a day or more to mould a very big pot (*palang*).
(iv) Allow to dry at room temperature for at least one week. More days may be required for larger pots.
(v) The items were then baked (*wenpit*) by placing selected grass (*kuwaal*) over the items, along with *mutkhii* (from silk cotton). Cow dung was then placed underneath and set on fire. When all the grass and cow dung were burnt, the items were allowed to cool and then tested by tapping each item by hand. Resonance of a good sound indicated that the process was successful. However, a queer sound indicated poor quality of the product.

Types of pots or items made included *yhibes, vhet, banggalang, yhi phimeh, kwalak, yhi khalang, Palang, tullmun, paii* (see figure 4.8), *yhitok, yhih, tull tok,* and *lhit.* These pots and other items were made to order or made in standard sizes and sold through trade by barter. Some were used as gift items, particularly to ladies who were preparing to marry or had recently married. Women and children made up the labour force for pot making. The children helped by carrying and grinding the clay. Pot making was a seasonal occupation which only occurred during the dry season.

Figure 4.8: Paih, used for fetching water or storing local beer (*Mwes*, or *burkutu* in Hausa).

4.11.4 Woodcarving: Woodcarving, practised mainly by men, was an individual affair, although assistance might be given by one or two other persons. Certain trees were highly favoured by woodcarvers for the production of different arts and crafts. Some of the products of woodcarving were traditional camp seats and stools. They were the same type produced by Tal people, whether in Gombe or Tal in Pankshin in Plateau State (see figure 4.9).

Figure 4.9: Traditional camp chair and stool (these are the same items used by Tal people in Gombe State and Pankshin LGA, Plateau State).

Table 4.4 displays the trees and plants produced:

Table 4.4: Types of trees or plants and products produced

S/NO	Names of Trees	Items Produced
1.	*Syeihyi*	Bed (*Kam, kin thin Khyan*, and *khong*)
2.	Mahogany (*Khok*)	Mortar and pestle (*Shing kin Hess*), drum (*Ninkhung*), and seats
3.	*Sen*	Mortar and pestle (*Shing kin Hess*) ladder
4.	*Dakyweng*	Seats, stools (*petong/ton Khong*), idols (*gyep tau*)
5.	*Yubi*	Bed (*kampan* and *khong*)
6.	*Bhet*	Ladder (*Seihyi*), mortar and pestle (*ting daak*)
7.	*Dep* (*Dinya*)	Drum (*Bang*)
8.	Tamarind (*Ras, Dhyis*)	Ladder (*Bal Shal, Seihyi*), hunting stick (*kampan*)
9.	*Gyelhit komduai*	Bow (*Rhyie*)

10.	*Khikam* (riverian special grass)	Arrows (*Kam Pas*)
11.	*Bhet*	*Daak* (game like *Ayo*, *Dara* in Hausa)
12.	*Ya'ah*	Handle of spear, roofing
13.	*Ting Kum* and *Theim*	Religious practise items (*Tau or kuk*), horn (*Bhwaat*)
14.	Bamboo (*Kweighat*)	Bed (*Paha-al*)
15.	Silk cotton (*Kheihyi*)	Cooking stick (*Kamyui*)

Source: Fieldwork, 2004

Most of the items produced and listed were for family use, but some were sold by trade and barter. Skills were widespread, as individuals specialised in the production of one or more of the items. Woodcarving was a seasonal occupation.

4.11.5 Weaving: Both men and women wove baskets. However, it was seen to be mostly a women's task. Materials used for this craft were *longpang*, *bhet*, and *bhuu* (also used for making mats, or *lesu*). These resources were readily available at home and within the river systems.

Tal people also wove special types of mats called *kalangang* using fresh desert palm (*borasus*) leaves. They wove local or traditional raincoats called *filip* using *kweighat* from fresh leaves. Men, women, and children were engaged in weaving *kyagang* from *gang* for dancing and bags called *beteh* and *kattim* from *ganggos* (a *borasus* subspecies).

Weaving was a flourishing traditional textile industry. Men and women used cotton to produce traditional clothing materials called *Thel* and *Thuun*, which were a triangular pant (*bante* in Hausa) used by men to cover their nakedness. A special bag called *tip theel* was highly cherished by men. It was used for especially important functions such as festivals, religious worship, farming, and hunting.

Weaving was a seasonal occupation; it was mostly done during the dry season. The items produced were mainly for family use, though some were made for sale by trade and barter. In some cases, they were produced based on request or order by interested parties.

4.12 Tal Traditional Architecture (House Building)

A typical traditional Tal house (see figure 4.10) had the design of a compound integrated with a circular layout, an open space arrangement in the middle and adjoining structures. There was one entrance, called *tayieh*. The traditional houses were round in nature. Each house had a specific utility factor. For instance, a compound consisted of the following structures:

Figure 4.10: A typical traditional Tal architecture of a compound integrated in nature. There is one entrance (*tayieh*) that leads into the other buildings with an open courtyard in the middle.

(i)   *Tayieh* and *balgam* were the entrance with *queih* (open space) which provided for a parlour where visitors could wait.
(ii)   *Kap-sang* was a male room.
(iii)   *Lu-tai mat* was a female room.
(iv)   *Lu-fin* was a milling or grinding room.
(v)   *Lu-mun* was the kitchen.

(i)   *Meh* was the granary.
(vii) *Dulum* was the brewing house.
(viii) *Gulut* was a lockout room, for private use only.
(ix) *Lubikhyeih* was the animal house.
(x)   *Bong khe* was the chicken house. This could be attached underneath the granary. In fact, a buildup could be made in such a way that cooking is done like a kitchen.
(xi) *Zhai* was an interlocking fence that joined each of the facility structures of a compound.

The materials used in house construction included stones (for laying the foundation), clay (for plastering), grass (for thatching), and timber (various forest tree products and *borasus* for roofing and decking).

The special sticky clay was mixed with straw and plant substances and pounded with *ghol*, for building construction. Foundation laying took a day or two. Production of blocks was not always necessary because as soon as the clay was ready, building commenced by hand. Layers were added two or three times daily. They depended very much on the weather for progress of the work. Another layer was added only when the previous one had dried properly.

4.13 Local beer making

Women were directly responsible for the production of a household's beer, called *mwes* (*burkutu* in Hausa).

The history of beer making is traceable to a man who had two wives. It happened that one of them was not good at cooking and was rejected by her husband. She was abandoned in the house. One day, while alone in her house during the rainy season, she dried guinea corn but forgot to take it in. Consequently, the corn was beaten by rain, and with time, it started germinating. However, the process of drying continued until one day she used it in cooking *yuaih* (gruel, *kunu* in Hausa). After preparing this drink, she sent for her husband's friend to come; when he came, she served him the drink. He enjoyed the drink so much and said the taste was fantastic and left. It became *mwes wet* (secret brewing).

51

She cooked the drink for a second time and sent for her husband's friend to come again. This time she invited her husband to come with him. The husband was reluctant but his friend persuaded him. The woman washed a calabash, fetched the drink, and served her husband's friend. He took up to three sips before giving it to the husband, who took it and was surprised to find it tasted so good.

When they finished what they were given, the husband told his friend to ask his wife if there was any more left ("*La ka shi bi ni ndiyeeh?*"). The friend refused but the husband persisted. The friend got up and asked her, "By the way, why did you invite me again?" In response, she said he was invited to come and have just one drink. Then he told her his friend wanted more, and she gave it to him.

With this discovery, the husband developed interest in his wife again. The drink (*mwes*) provided a tonic for unity and the renewal of marital relationship and lasting friendship. As his friend stood up to go, he instructed him to tell his son to bring his *khong* or *petai* (bed) for him. He said he would not go back home that day. Thus, the accidental discovery marked the genesis of local beer brewing in Tal.

As the woman continued cooking this drink, other women learned the process from her, and it became widely spread in the community as *mwes wet,* before it became commercial.

The amount and frequency with which beer was brewed did not depend on wealth and standing of the family. What mattered was availability of the grains in a household. Then beer could be brewed for sale, for workers on the farm, or to mark the celebration of an event or a sign of happiness.

Beer was brewed by the following process:

(i)   Pound the grain, corn, or millet (*Mwahtu*).
(ii) Soak the grain, corn, or millet (*Qhue'eh*).
(iii) Wash the corn on the third day (*Wap Suwa'ah*).
(iv) *Mwanshiep Kin yak ham* (collect firewood and fetch water) on the fourth day.
(v)   Grind the grain on the fifth day (*Sam*).

(vii) Boil the grounded grain on the sixth day (*Fhuel*).

(vii) *Gyim* (this is the "eve of the beer" on the seventh day).

(viii) *Nung* (the beer is ready for consumption on the eighth day).

Beer was highly regarded in the community. It was taken as a kind of status symbol for notables or well-to-do persons in the society like the *Miskom Dil* or *Gwolong Kum* (chief priest). The sweetened part (before fermentation), called *gyim,* was served as a local beverage to women and children. *Dangmen* could also be produced by using the by-product of *fhiss sam* (*dusa*) left in a big pot (*palang*) soaked with water, and then added to the *gyim*, cooked, served, and drank after cooling.

4.14 Trade and Exchange

Trade by barter was organised by Tal people among themselves and other non-natives such as Ngas, from Garram, Wukkos, or Pankshin and Hausa traders from Katsina. Units of measurement were baskets and calabashes. However, in some instances bundles of grains could be exchanged for a particular crop or food item. For example, a bundle of guinea corn was exchanged with a basket of groundnuts. Also, a bottle of mahogany oil was exchanged for either a bundle of millet or guinea corn. Local Maggie was exchanged for millet or groundnuts.

The same trade by barter was extended to livestock. A bundle of guinea corn was exchanged for a female goat, sheep, or cow. One basket of groundnuts or bambra nuts was exchanged for the purchase of livestock. Most of the transactions were done at the household level, but later on it was extended to the markets when they became established.

If a household ran short of a particular item, it was obtained by exchange of one commodity for another. These local exchanges were done face to face by barter. Later, cowrie shells (see figure 4.11) were introduced and served as a local standard and acceptable legal tender currency. For instance, it was used for business or trading transactions. Cowrie shells were used to purchase foodstuff, livestock, or cloth (traditionally woven material such as Thuun, Thel, or even payment of the bride price). Furthermore, they could be used to buy fifty-kilogram bags of salt, one bundle of millet or guinea corn or goat, sheep, or cow. According to one of the informants, the shells were brought from Awe and Azara in the present Nasarawa State of Nigeria.

Goods not produced by the community, such as mineral salt, were obtained from Mernyang or Kwaklak (Kwalla) people in what is now Qua'anpan LGA in Plateau State. These people obtained salt from Azara, Awe, and Akiri (all in present-day Nasarawa State) and brought it to Tal. In exchange, they were given *khyan* (hoe), *thun*, and *bi-piya* (traditionally woven clothing material).

There were no local markets. Besides, the prevailing situations of war and the lack of security and safety prevented the possibility of establishing formal points for marketing, commerce, trade, and exchange.

Apart from barter, as noted above, a kind of currency that had reached Tal was cowrie shells (*Hasnamwet*). See figure 4.11. They were used by the people during the precolonial period. There was no trade in slaves to the lowlands; rather, Tal people paid for the import of slaves. There were exceptional cases during famine when a person was sold in exchange for food when no food could be found in the family.

Figure 4.11: Cowrie shells (*Hasnamwet*) for payment of dowry and legal tender for buying, selling, and trading during the precolonial regime.

4.15 Social Organisation

Tal people lived according to clan affiliation and locality of groups. They considered themselves as members of one stock, with a common place of origin, held together based on a consensus of tacit agreement on culture, basic rules, norms, values, beliefs, morals, tradition, and social order. Matters under constant review were deviant behaviours, social relationships, uniformities of social interactions and patterns, and expected behaviour towards one's neighbours in everyday life.

By reference, a social organisation can be defined as the coordination of social relationships among persons or groups, so that they can function effectively in the society. This can be seen or viewed in three aspects: structure, process, and function.

a. Structure is a network of relationship that connects status and roles in general. For example, the role of parents and children in a family setting and their overall functions or contributions towards societal well-being.

b. Process is the adoption of social relationships and functions to the ever-changing needs of the group or society. The response could be due to physical or environmental factors. For instance, disputes over land resource utilisation could be settled by a general sitting (*na'anshang*) for judgement (*yaghol*) and towards peaceful resolution of the conflict. This was how disagreements or quarrels were often settled between Tal and Angas, with Wedu recognised as the principal senior arbitrator.

c. Function concerns the division of labour, allocation of duties, and social differentiation of status and roles in the society.

4.16 Kinship Terminology

Kinship refers to relationship by blood and similarity in character. Based on this definition, kinship (matrilineal) terminology of Tal people was as listed below:

i. *Khin:* mother's parents or relations
ii. *Khinsot* or *yaset*: first cousins (*guang*)

iii. *Hemnin* or *hemnhang*: brother or sister of the same father and mother, or same father but different mothers or same mother but different fathers

iv. *Latom*: grandfather

v. *Latom gu tubis*: great-grandfather

vi. *Khakha*: grandmother

vii. *Khakha gu tubis*: great-grandmother

viii. *Gigyep*: children

ix. *Lilah*: child (male or female)

x. *Layep*: daughter

xi. *Hem*: son (*la miskhom*, boy/son)

xii. *Dah*: father (grandparent on the father's side)

xiii. *Nang*: mother (grandparent on the mother's side)

It is important to note that *khin* is a universal umbrella and is used in defining the matriarchal lineage from the first to the tenth or even up to the twentieth generation. Thus, there could be an overlap in the houses with regards to relationships.

4.17 Clan and Lineage Structure

As noted earlier, clan and lineage structure was based on matrilineal decent. The tradition has been maintained within the major clans of Tal, Zak, and Yong. People lived together according to clan affiliation and nuclear families in compounds, as shown in figure 4.12.

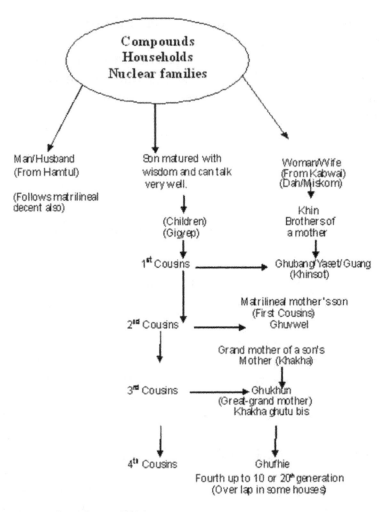

Source: Field Survey, 2004.

Figure 4.12. Family lineage up to fourth, tenth, or twentieth generations.

4.18 Marriage

Marriage in Tal is a traditionally recognised institution of the union of a woman and man, cohabiting as husband and wife. Tal people practised the following types of marriages: polygamy, monogamy, and levirate.

- Polygamy: a marriage system where a man married more than one wife.

- Monogamy: Marriage of one man, one wife; both traditional and Christian religions practice this.
- Levirate: Variant of polygamous practice. According to traditional practice, a man could inherit or take the wife of his deceased brother, known as *tsemun mat khop hemnhinna*. In some cases, it could be any other relation from the father's or mother's side. However, the consent of the woman was very important. If she disapproved of the relationship, no marriage would take place.

4.18.1 Modes of Marriage

Traditionally, there were different ways under which marriage could be contracted:

a. **Capture by force** (*yep yhah*). If a young man was in love with a woman and she did not love him, but her parents liked the man, he could secretly arrange with his friends to take her by force in the market or wine place. As soon as this happened, her parents were notified by a mediator within twenty-four hours. An arrangement for payment of the dowry was done later. If he was lucky, she would stay. But she might escape at the slightest opportunity.

b. **Elopement** (*su whet*). If the girl loved her suitor and the parents disapproved of the relationship for marriage, they could plan together secretly that the girl would disappear and follow her lover to his house without the knowledge of the girl's parents. A mediator would be sent to notify the parents about what had happened. When this was done, final settlement would be done to fulfil all the traditional conditions acceptable to both parties.

c. **Exchange** (*yhaap phim*). Two young men could exchange their sisters for marriage, with the consent and arrangement between the parents of the two families. But there was a great disadvantage here. For instance, if there was a quarrel or misunderstanding and one of the sisters left, the other sister had to come back to cook food for her brother, no matter how peaceful her own marriage was, until her brother's wife returned or was brought back.

d. Mutual agreement (*su fwung*). This was consensus marriage by consideration of a young girl and boy who felt deeply touched and loved each other. They went about courtship and dated each other in a traditional way. Young people often kept many friends, so that when the time came, the best was selected for marriage. Parents did not interfere because if they suggested a husband or wife for their children and something happened, they would be held responsible. They would, however, offer advice on how to make a good choice. At the appropriate time, the parents of the girl gave a date to all those who had shown interest in their daughter to bring what could be accepted as part of the dowry. When all of them had assembled, the girl was called out to choose the young man she loved and wanted to marry. She would hold the items from the hands of the father of her suitors. This action indicated that the chapter was closed. The other contestants had to carry their items home. With this development, the parents of the lucky man would then make arrangement by fixing a date to complete all formalities of payment of the rest of the dowry. If the girl was pretty, of good character, and industrious, the dowry was paid in full, or even with extra. But if she wasn't beautiful, of bad character, or lazy, only the fixed price was paid.

4.18.2 Dowry or Bride Price Payment

During the precolonial period, payment of dowry consisted of the following:

(i) Three large hoes (*kyan long, Kasul, Khumes*). The smallest is Khum-es used for cleaning excreta (see figure 4.13a).

(ii) Three bundles of traditionally woven material (*thel thuun*).

(iii) Twelve goats, one as *yabal* and one as *yelfung*. The size of the biggest animals must be such that three fingers can go through the nose. Sheep were also accepted from those who didn't have goats.

Figure 4.13a. Three large hoes used for bride price
payment in Tal during the colonial period.

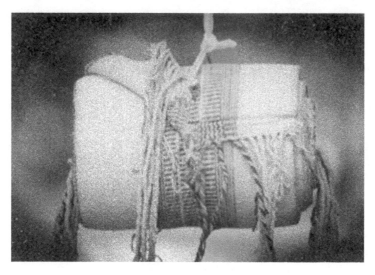

Figure 4.13b. Traditional woven material (*Tehl*)
used for dowry or payment of bride price.

Since society is dynamic, payment became modernised during the post-colonial period. Dowry was paid using animals as well as hard currency. Three big goats, nine sheep, and eight to twenty pounds sterling (£8 to £20) cash were required (Dilkon, 1967). However, in 1957, during the reign of Chief Adamu Gutus Mutkhai, the use of large hoes for payment of dowry stopped, and it was replaced with twenty pounds payment, introduced to cover for the animals (goats/sheep) in 1957. Some areas still accept either three goats or nine sheep. One goat was sometimes given as *kwuamwui* (courtship) and not recognised as part of the dowry.

4.19 Engagement Steps and Marriage Period

If intending partners agreed, the courtship was therefore recognised and formalised. The period of engagement was from January to August. The marriage period began in August and lasted to the middle of October. This timeframe allowed the parents to harvest their crops, especially guinea corn. By tradition, the father was expected to give twenty bundles of guinea corn to his daughter, while the brothers of her mother were to give ten bundles or so. The situation depended on the economic circumstances of the parents and uncles of the bride. Most ladies did not want to be rushed into marriage outside the set marriage period. If the suitor insisted, she would ask, "Am I pregnant?" ("*Ah Yeh ghi gam ah?*") If she included the phrase "*A tieh bina a khit su khet,*" this means he was rejected.

The following steps were taken to formalise relationships leading to marriage:

(i)   Participation in a dance known as *Dideng* (African blues), which was a kind of courtship dance, where females and males selected each other. The males filed up as they danced with the selected females, who followed their men, chanting loving words in the songs. At a point, the males turned to face their selected girls, putting their two hands on the ladies' shoulders, chanting loving words to lure the girls into intimate acceptance of them as they danced. The female normally responded to their man. Each man and woman communicated in his or her own varied ways as the dance went on. As soon as the dance ended, each male was involved in a love discussion with his selected lady, depending on his skill on the dancing floor. As they danced, they sang and coaxed each other and made loving statements about their families and themselves. It was a very pleasant song meant to touch their feelings or hearts.

(ii)   As a follow-up, they would meet again at a dancing place. The male interested in the girl would pay a visit to her in the house, to tell her his intentions. If she agreed, courtship began.

(iii) The courtship period lasted for about three years. During the three years, the suitor was expected to work on her parents' farm. So when the father brewed *mwes* for farming, the suitor would invite all his mates, males and females, to go and work on the farm of his fiancé's parents. This was called *maizelet* or *ta shieu*. With this, a steady relationship was built.

While the courtship went on, if both parties loved each other and wanted to get married, an intermediary (*guyei*) was selected. This was usually a relative (*khin*).

The suitor usually went with one of his best friends during courtship (*kuwham*), but on some occasions he would go alone. A confirmation of the friendship was done by the intermediary. If the outcome was positive (*shik zang*), the man went back the second time to further confirm the promise. If there was no change of mind, a relation of the father was sent to inform the parents of the prospective bride that they were coming on a certain date.

On the appointed date, the boy's parents would go in company of the *guyei*. At this meeting an agreement would be reached on the payment of the dowry. The suitor's family would be told what to bring or pay. Another date was set for this transaction. When the day came, the boy's parents would come fully prepared. Before the payment was made, any problem or offence against the girl's parents or relatives would be resolved. A fine was usually paid by a goat or two. It had to be amicably resolved before the acceptance of the dowry.

The issue of payment of the dowry was then transacted by exchange of the items mentioned earlier. When the items were received, the parents returned home and informed other family members that it was done successfully. Beauty, hard work, and good character, among other attributes, were used to determine how much was to be paid by a father-in-law.

In some cases, after the payment of dowry, the girl would say she had something else pending (*La kwabi ndinpna d ye-mai pubnamwa*). That is, "There is still something before me to be done, such as work on my father's farm." Her suitor would then mobilise people to come and work on her parents' farm. It was usually done as a mark of happiness and called *mai na'a mang*.

Having fulfilled all righteousness, their engagement started any time between January and August. Arrangements for marriage were made. The uncle of the girl (the mediator) would fix the date, usually from September to October. Her mother would choose a well-behaved woman and a girl to escort her daughter. The woman was called *mat-shyell*. Two young men and two young ladies from the bridegroom's side would go to the house of the girl in the evening, between eight and nine o'clock. When they all assembled at the father's house, the girl and the two men from the suitor's village would go in and receive her before leaving. When she came out, she would kneel down, pretending that she didn't want to go. The men would beg, plead, and persuade her to go with them. Eventually, she would agree to get up and follow them.

The journey continued until they came quite close to the compound of the husband-to-be. Then she would immediately kneel down (*shangkwet ka phifim ya*), and the flower girl (*layep gu shell*) would be by her side, at a distance of about a hundred metres. She would walk on her knees until she entered the house. Upon their arrival, all the people in the compound would come out. There the girl would be adamant and refuse to enter the house. The two young men would forcefully carry her inside. In most instances, the people usually had to plead, welcome her, and ask her to get up and go into the house. Only *mat-shell* would remain with her for some time. All the others would go back home. The woman stayed to advise her on all aspects of married life before leaving her alone with her husband.

Her father must have given her at least thirty bundles of guinea corn in addition to another twenty-five or thirty expected from her husband's house to start a living. That is why all marriages had to be done at harvest periods to enable parents send their daughters with enough foodstuff, especially guinea corn and millet.

4.20 Criteria for Marriage

In Tal, the average age for a young lady to get married was eighteen. There was no age limit for the boys. What mattered most were his maturity, wisdom, and ability to withstand hardship. If his parents noticed that he could withstand the rigours of working very hard from morning to evening (6 a.m. to 5 p.m.), it was assumed that he was mature and responsible and could marry. If a woman's first child was a male, and the second was also a male, the first-born usually married first. However, this did not always happen. If the first son was not handsome, was unlucky, or was not admired by ladies, *yaapmwa bal kha mhip* (the second-born) could be allowed to marry first.

If there were girls as third—and fourth-born, when they grew up and got married, their dowries would be used for paying the dowry of their brothers' wives. In a situation where the first three children were males and the fourth was a girl, it was believed the first son did not want a girl, so a son was born. For this, he had to work very hard to earn money or the means to pay the dowry of his own wife (Dilkon, 1967).

The question of who to marry was very clear. Tal people did not permit marriages to take place between very close family relatives. Marriages were only allowed outside a person's immediate family. Also, trial marriages were not allowed.

4.20.1 Virginity

One of the most important cultural values which the people of Tal cherished was the issue of chastity and virginity. Society was concerned with the behaviour and movement of unmarried young men and women. They could play and do any other thing apart from having sexual intercourse.

Both parties were very conscious of the consequences premarital sex would have on them in future, when they got married. So they were careful about how to relate with each other by avoiding touching each other. The man did not want to get close to the woman because of what lies ahead after marriage, should they cross the line. Thus, if the boy and girl were very close, they would be disgraced in the future, after they married. For instance, if a terrible disease attacked the bride or her child or baby, the old woman who escorted the girl to her marriage home would interrogate her. She would ask her if she had contact with any man when she was a girl. Sex outside wedlock, known as *tillet,* was forbidden.

Another problem could be if she experienced difficulty with delivery or was not able to conceive. The girl had to respond to the old woman's questions. The woman would ask her to name all the men she ever had sexual intercourse with before marriage. If it was more than one, she had to go to all of them and get a he-goat from each of them. No argument was expected on this payment.

The goats were to be sacrificed to the idols of her father in order to appease the gods. Through the seers, consultations would be made according to tradition to determine the cause of the sickness or disease in question. If they said it was fornication that was the cause of the baby's sickness, the girl must quickly go to the man and collect (ihyi tillet) one he-goat. If the man delayed and the child died, the corpse would be brought to his door and left there. This would require him to pay a heavier fine before the child was buried.

4.21 Purpose of Marriage

As a young man grew up, he would look for a girl to marry. The primary reasons for marriage among Tal people were

- to have children;
- to find a helper for cooking food;
- to have an assistant in farming;
- to have companionship and satisfy the biological need for sexual intercourse; and
- to be accepted in the society among equals.

There was a belief that a person who was not married would not get rich. Even if he was rich, nobody would inherit his wealth, riches, or property.

4.22 Divorce (Termination of Marriage)

A marriage between a man and woman could be dissolved or terminated. The case had to be proved beyond reasonable doubt according to traditional ways of investigation to establish or ascertain the truth. The most common grounds for divorce were

i.   stealing;
ii.   gross misconduct, such as being rude or exhibiting bad character, unusual behaviour, or disobedience;
iii. adultery, fornication (unfaithfulness), or involvement in witchcraft; or
iv.   brutality

When a man divorced his wife, she could go back to her parents and live with them while she looked for another husband. But there was an unwritten law that forbade anyone in the village from marrying her (Dilkon, 1967). This was especially true if it was an established case of witchcraft or inherited disease such as leprosy (*kwop*).

4.23   Organisation of the Household

A typical household comprises of a man, woman, children, and relatives residing together in a compound setting. The children could be married but stay with their parents. The people of Tal usually did not stay in the same compound with their adult brothers and family. Whenever a man got married, he had to leave and build his own compound or house and stay with his wife. If he had more than one wife, he must build houses for each of them separately in the same compound. He would rotate his visitation (sleeping period) among the women for a specified time in order to avoid quarrels and to ensure cooperation among the wives during farming work.

If the man had two or three wives and one of them was without a child, by arrangement, she could take one from any of the other wives to stay with her.

The husband headed the family. His wife or wives must be answerable to him. The children and their mothers must obey him and girls must obey boys, even though they are from the same family. Food is shared according to age. Seniority was maintained among the wives. If the man had many wives, the first acted as the head of the household, and the other wives must obey her. Whenever there was a dispute within a household and the matter was beyond the husband's capability, elders were called upon to intervene and resolve the conflict amicably.

A typical household in Tal is represented by figure 4.14.

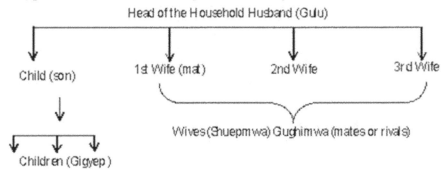

Figure 4.14. Household organisation in Tal.

The diagram illustrates a household of one person with three wives and a grown-up son with his own children (*gigyep*), all living together. Each of the wives must have her own house.

Organisation of the household was based on mutual understanding and the basic sense of accepting responsibility at any given time. For family problems involving husbands, wives, or children accused of any misdemeanour, murder, or witchcraft, immediate action was usually taken. First cousins (sons of *khinsot*) were always informed first. What they said determined what action was to be taken: execution or banishment (excommunication) from the village.

References

Dafwan, Pubyen (2011). Provided samples of cowrei shells on 28/11/2011. Aged 27 years.

Dilkon, W. W. (1967). "An Outline of Tal Culture." Unpublished document.

Focus Groups (2003). From randomly selected localities interviewed using structured questionnaire on 26/01/2003. Provided information on all the different aspects of the chapter:

Yepkung-Kabwai (male), age 50 years.
Kinkop-Kyam (male), age 49 years.
Dangvwang-Kwashi (male), age 61 years.
Khungshel-Mudong (male), age 53 years.
Mutshel Lafot-Kwopzak (male), age 55 years.
Toma Tashik-Hamtul (male), age 45 years.
Mwangyes Guyit-Kabwai (male), age 67 years.
Wakrang-Kyam (male), age 53 years.

Gupiya, Ambrose B. (2003). Tal chief (*Gwolong*). Interviewed on 08/03/2003 on trade and exchange. Age 50 years.

Kaklai-Khiling (2003). Informant interviewed on 16/08/2003 on iron smelting, blacksmithing, weaving, woodcarving, pottery, traditional architecture, and beer brewing. Age 61 years.

Kopzak, Luka L. Talya (2003). Informant interviewed on 08/03/2003 on Tal marriage processes and formalisation traditions. Age 53 years.

Kungmang, Tudil (2011). Interviewed on 22/01/2011 on the organisation of trade by barter in Tal. Aged 65 years.

Lafot, Mutshel (2003). Informant interviewed on 16/08/2003 on iron smelting and blacksmithing. Age 58 years.

Langa, Adamu (2003). Informant interviewed on 26/01/2003. Migrant in Nakwan, Shendan Local Government Area, provided information on Tal precolonial marriage systems. He is from Vonrong (Takhong) in Tal. Age 90-plus years.

Mangkhung (2003). Informant interviewed on 28/03/2003 on hunting. Age 65 years.

Rumtong, Mitok Yakubu (2004). Informant residing in Jos. Interviewed on 28/04/2004 on hunting, crop storage, trade and exchange, precolonial social organisation, farming, land tenure system, and marriage. Age 90-plus years.

Tal Community Development Association (1988). "Five Hundred Thousand Naira (N500, 000) Development Appeal Fund Programme Pankshin," pp. 12-13.

Wakrang (2003). Informant interviewed on 16/08/2003 on traditional crafts, textiles, traditional cottage industry, and cloth weaving. Age 60 years.

Yating, Bitrus (2003). Informant residing at Tal-Lawuya, interviewed on 03/02/2003. Provided information on forest products, uses, and economic values of trees in Tal. Age 60 years.

Youbamson, Emmanuel L. (2004). Informant based in Jos, from Khongbalam (Zemsu). Interviewed on 24/08/2004 on precolonial social organisation social structure and order of Tal people. Age 50 years.

Chapter Five

Traditional Tal Religion

5.0 Introduction

Tal Cosmology. This chapter focuses on the religious world-view of the Tal people. Understanding their world-view provides the basis for understanding who they are and what they can and cannot do. It also explains how they relate with the natural environment and interpret events, what controls the basic fabric of life in their socio-cultural organisation, their view of life in relation to the universe, and their philosophy of the dynamics of human activities here on earth.

It is the opinion of the author that one of the best ways to understand Tal people is through their traditional religion, culture, agricultural activities, socio-economic, and political organisation because these are a reflection of their general world-view. This is confirmed by scholars who posit that a world-view seeks to answer fundamental questions about the place and relationship of man with the universe. Answers to these fundamental questions provide us with the blueprint for controlling our environment and for establishing our social and political institutions. Conversely, knowledge of a people's world-view is a key to understanding their social, political, and even psychological problems (Ikenga-Metuh, cited in Gwamna, 1996, p. 56).

5.1 The Supreme Being

According to the traditional religious belief of the Tal people, the supreme being was Na'an, who had supernatural power. They believed he had total control over the earth and the universe, such as the power to do and undo the alpha and omega, being in total control of all life situations here on earth and in the hereafter, after we exited from the earth. Just like other African animists, they believed in the existence of only one God, the supreme ruler of the world, but they frankly admitted little knowledge about his attributes (Meek, 1931). At death they believed God received people's souls. They believed in reincarnation. Conscious efforts were made to maintain a close relationship with God so as to derive maximum benefits. As a mark of respect and reverence to the supreme being, he was not worshiped directly. He was considered to be too powerful for them to confront or go to directly.

Tal people described God in both genders, depending on circumstances. Na'an was described as a female due to the issue of fertility. A lot of respect was given to the supreme being such that the people did not swear or use God's name in vain. Swearing was done only when there was a serious issue at stake; for instance, when someone was accused of witchcraft or having committed murder for which there was no direct evidence. Therefore, they devised how to worship him through the following intermediaries:

- The *Na'anshang* was a ceremony of thanksgiving to God for bringing out children successfully from the shrine during the circumcision/initiation ceremony.
- *Mukweikum* was an ancestral-cultist who talked directly to God. He interceded on behalf of the clan and the entire Tal nation.
- Some individuals were identified to have direct link or access to talk to God.
- Sacred images or idols, such as an object stone (*Pang na'an*), were used as a medium of communication with God. It could also be a wooden image like *Tau*.

5.2 The Ancestral Spirits

The Tal people's ancestral worship covered all forms of cult of the dead, which was the predominating influence for the cult of *Kum* or *Dodo* (tutelary genius and physical representation of the spiritual) (Meek, 1931). Ancestor worship was based on the universal belief in life after death of the human soul. Men and women who lived to a good old age were believed to have a vigorous soul; when they went to the next world, they took with them spiritual power and could assist their tribe and protect their people. This explains why when a man died outside Tal, his head and bones were taken back home for burial.

Any person (male or female) who died could become an ancestor. It was particularly important for a woman's spirit to make the excursion back to her ancestral home. It was believed that the spirit of the dead (*tut*) stayed in the shrine or somewhere suitable. Tal people believed that they possessed great powers and kept watch over them. They supposedly brought good things and protected them against evil forces. If there was any evil plan among the living, the spirits were believed to intervene so that nothing tragic happened.

Ancestors acted as intermediaries between man and God. Masquerades were believed to be ancestral spirits, so it was necessary to keep them happy. This was done by offering sacrifices using goats or chickens and liquor (*mwes*). A drop of *mwes* and the blood of the slaughtered animal were placed at the tomb. If a chicken was used, the feathers were plucked and fixed or dropped on the tomb. The goats were used for *fwa'an*. The most senior person in the family, *miskom kum,* was in charge of incantation of the ancestors (*fwa'an, kakhyi,* and *tau*). But for the entire Tal community, *Mwandok, Khuwaih,* and *Na'an* were in charge. A shrine was maintained and regular sacrifices were made. The sacrifices were made by the most senior male.

5.3   Lesser Deities

Apart from the belief in the existence of a supreme being, Tal people had lesser deities who were physically represented by idols or wooden images. Thus, deification of actual phenomena (naturalism) and attribution of a spirit to material objects (fetishism and spiritism) was practised. They believed that lesser deities are servants (small gods) of the supreme being, so requests were channelled through them to him. These lesser deities included the following:

(i)   *Mwandok* (chief masquerade)
(ii)   *Nwong*
(iii)   *Shirii*
(iv)   *Khuwaih*
(v)   Fwa'an
(vi)   *Gyen* (responsible for the spirit of twins)
(vii) *Tau*

(viii) *Tongzhing*

(ix) *Vet Thyi* (performs almost the same function as *Gyen*; parents were punished for any unjust treatment of twins)

(x) *Mangap*

(xi) *Gongsel*

Lesser deities were associated with certain powers, such as the following:

(i) **Mwandok:** The main function of *Mwandok* was to handle all cases of epidemics, unusual or suspicious deaths, evil spirits, or other circumstances which were considered unnatural by the people. *Mwandok* had the power to cause the disease or epidemic; aspirations were poured in the name of its god to forestall future occurrences. *Mwandok* also caused leprosy. He was regarded as the god of judgement and carried out capital punishment for any wrong thing done such as murder, stealing, or passing excreta in water systems or rivers.

(ii) **Fwa'an** was believed to possess the power to handle sicknesses associated with women. For instance, any woman who had committed a serious offence could have irregular menstruation or her child could develop scurvy, become dehydrated (*nuwaih*), or have a back ache. When this happened, *Fwa'an* was called to intercede in order to appease the god offended. The woman had to confess her sin.

(iii) **Nwong** (Dodo, tutelary genius): *Nwong* was believed to dispense judgement based on the people's belief. It had powers to cause rheumatism (*qwayak sai kin shii*), arthritis, and swelling of the stomach (*wuup*).

(iv) **Shirii's** power caused boils and infertility among women. So it required an investigation (*khespaah*) to ascertain what was wrong. It caused *wuup,* mainly among men, and they had to bathe before it disappeared. For women, it could cause irregular menstruation or repeated abortion.

(v) **Khuwaih** was believed to have powers to cause retention of stool (*wuup*) within twenty-four hours. If no confession was made, the person was likely to die. Complete revelation was required before the person was cured. When it was chronic, *ihyen khuaih* was administered.

(vi) **Gongsel** was believed to cause a permanent cancer on the cheek. It was incurable until a confession was made and the gods were appeased.

(vii) **Tau** was believed to possess power of fertility and infertility. So if a woman did something wrong, her child could develop skin disease. The infection could only be cured if *Tau* was appeased. The woman could not even conceive, unless a sacrifice had been made. If it happened when she was pregnant, when she gave birth to the child, he would either be infected with a skin disease or be malnourished or dehydrated (*nuwaih*).

(viii) Other deities like **Gyen** took care of the spirit of twins and offered protection against diarrhoea, migraine, and insanity.

(ix) **Tongzhing** had no special powers but was an intermediary between children and the supreme being. He was a symbol of the bravery of children.

(x) **Vet Thyi** was also believed to have powers to protect people against migraine and insanity.

(xi) **Mangap** was a kind of social cult. People became members through *vwang* (initiation) as men of substance (*miskom*). At social functions, especially where liquor was brewed, they tasted the liquor before any other person. Any person who got initiated became dependent on the initiator, who would find a wife for him. When he died, only his cult members (*mangap*) would bury him. All his property belonged to the membership, not to his family.

Mangap was powerless and harmless. However, to a great extent, members had some powers related to rain making, which controlled agriculture and prosperity of the community. The identity of members was not hidden because they all carry long walking sticks (*dayi*) with two heads, a local bag (*tipshak*), and locust bean leaves. Membership was very strict. If the initiator gave somebody anything and he took it, the person automatically became a member. But if he refused, a fine had to be paid. Even if someone touched or crossed over the stick, the person became a member. They were noted to have great influence on *fwhen* and *kyel* (rain making and rain stopping).

(xii) **Fwhen** (rain making) and **kyel** (rain stopping) usually involved wind storms (*kheiyem*). The people of Takhong were known to be experts and possessed powers for rain making or stopping. However, before one had the power to make this happen, the following conditions had to be met:

(i) From March to April and July to August, the man totally abstained from having sexual intercourse (his wives included).

(ii) He must follow a specific diet. He must not eat draw soup containing *dakweng* (a wild vegetable tree flower), *tokna'an*, *mes* (locust beans), or *maaih* (fresh millet) in particular.

(iii) He was never to travel with a woman known to be menstruating.

There were three *fwhen* (rain making) pots with a special precious stone, shining, hook-like metal, and crystal clear (like diamonds). Once the leader had done all the mixing, he then left it with young boys. These boys were virgins taught by him to make the rain in his absence.

Tal people did not have priests drawn from particular families in charge of lesser deities. The most senior men (*miskom kum*) of the lineage were always the custodians of the various deities. This role was rotational (*tungdeh*) in the family.

Spirits (*Nyenpemwa, bhimwa, khikyang, mhimhilimwa,* and *fer piyha*). Tal people had various kinds of spirits. Some of these spirits were good and played very significant roles in the lives of the people. There were particular locations where they were found, such as rivers, rocks, or trees.

According to oral traditions, their operations were not in doubt because of some incidences that occurred. For example, around the nineteenth century, one day a group of Jihadists (*Tubi*) came to Pangfwhen (*Hamtul*) from Bauchi through Shendam and stayed under the hill in the evening with the aim of launching a surprise attack (Jihad) on the people. But that evening, there was a heavy downpour of rain, and the spirits of the rocks spoke to each other about these strangers. Unsatisfied with their presence, one large solid rock suddenly descended and rolled on them, and only one escaped death.

Oral tradition has it that Mernyang people (from the then Shendam Division, now Qua'anpan LGA) came to steal horses in Tal. It was asserted that when they reached Panglang (rock formation), Nyenphemwa and Bhimwa advised them to wait for a meeting with the Tal people in the evening, but they refused and so could not move with the horses.

Another example of the power of the spirits associated with rivers was that of River Kyafyhen. If a new bride was married in the community, the *gubwon* (leader) had to go and inform the river that the community had a stranger. If this was not done, and the bride went to fetch water with other ladies or women, as she placed her pot or container to fetch the water, she would disappear into the river and would not return home.

In the same River Kyafyhen, near Langzok, one day there was a call for people to assemble by the river. It was discovered that a crocodile was making a lot of noise and preventing women from fetching water. Other cases were reported at Konggang. The *Gwolong Kum* (chief-priest) wanted to know why this was happening. The next day, Bedung, chief of Tal, became sick, and he died later in the year. Some people asserted that the crocodile was the shadow (*vhip*) of a man who had been killed by somebody.

The areas where spirits lived were surrounded by taboos. For instance, women under menstruation were banned from passing there. If they did, their menses would not stop until they confessed and the leader of the spirits appeased. For places like Pangfwhen, Lasweng, Zawa, and Phyitei, it was forbidden to touch the ground with a walking stick. Nobody was allowed to cut any tree at that vicinity. Any disobedience resulted in sicknesses, and refusal to confess culminated in death. The same applied to the trees surrounding the rocks at Kabyak. No fire could burn them or be brought near them at night. Anyone who failed to observe the taboos would be infected with *ndwang* (smallpox) or even die. This could extend to the whole family. His children could contract measles (*hemlet* or *nasuk*).

5.4 Masquerades

Tal people had masquerades, but women were banned from seeing them in the open. This was because they were spirits (*Nhogubismwa*) representing God. The principal masquerades included the following:

(i) Mwandok

This spirit wore a mask and robed its body with a reddish-brown substance, called *zhanglip*, adorned with different colours. It appeared when there was a great problem in the community or when a prominent person died. This was the most dreaded masquerade, noted for exercising instant judgement in the form of capital punishment. It beat people and was very harsh. It dealt ruthlessly with people, especially on issues like witchcraft. It was the most powerful spirit. When it appeared, the rest ran away. It has been asserted that *Mwandok* was the spirit of wicked people who had died. It was known as the god of judgement.

(ii) Khiyim

This spirit announced its presence by blowing a trumpet (traditional animal horn). It came out during the millet harvest period. It moved around to protect the millet from theft. It appeared in a kind of evergreen woven-like attire, using a traditional wild magic plant called *tatakhating*, which looked like green thread. The roots could not be easily seen or traced by anybody. The body was also decorated with bamboo leaves (*kweighat*); this masquerade originated in Thel and Shendam. It came out between July and August. This was a period of hard work for women and children, collecting a lot of animal waste to have enough organic fertiliser for the next farming season. When he came to a house or compound and noticed there was no fodder for the animals, he gave instruction to provide it immediately. Failure to comply attracted severe punishment. Quarrels between husband

and wife or women rivalling over a man were not tolerated. This was known by him without being told. *Khiyim* came from Damhyi, Kyam, Mudong, Tangge, Koptaan, Hamtul, and Kabyak.

(iii) Nwong

(*Kum maaih*) came out in August, usually in the morning during millet harvest period. It disturbed people greatly. It appeared in material from raffia palms and tree leaves. The origin was from Wullum in Garram.

(iv) **Kumphis**

This masquerade was purely concerned with entertainment and merriment. The origin was from Kwaklak. It also dressed in raffia-woven leaves. It came out occasionally.

(v) **Kutdang** was known as *ass* (dog) of tutelary genius. It operated within the shrine and frightened women and children.

5.5   Witches and Witchcraft

Witches (*gusetmwa*) possessed both negative and positive powers (i.e. they had protective as well as destructive or harmful powers). It was believed that witches had powers to appease the spirits, and this relationship was used to either protect someone or kill them. Witches were believed to harm people through the spirit world and by nocturnal activities.

Those who were accused of being witches were believed to be harmful and thought to get it at birth. Thus, being a witch was hereditary and not by initiation. Witches operated in groups and rotated meeting venues. Witches were supposed to offer a member of their family in rotation (*tungdeh*). Failure to do so resulted in the death of the witch. It was not only members of their immediate families that the witches would harm or kill, but also from their lineage or clan.

Activities of witches and witchcraft were not left unchecked. There were procedures for detecting and punishing witches. A person with *fung*, a natural or special ability (third eye), or a medicine man could detect witches. The procedures of investigation included sorcery (*kespa'ah*) and involuntary confession by the witch (*guse'et*). If it was confirmed or established that someone was a witch, while the sick person was still alive, the witch would be asked to release or set the sick person free. A fine of six goats or one cow had to be paid. But if the sick person died, either of the following punishments could be administered:

(1)   the witch was excommunicated or banished from the community for life; or

(2)   the witch was killed. Capital punishment, according to customs and traditional practice of *na'antep* or *mwandok mang*, was administered if the case was determined to be very serious.

Other people accused of being witches were those identified by gifted people (third-eyed people) or medicine men (*Gu Hyenmwa*) in the community.

Apart from witches, other persons used medicine to harm others by using *wom* or *bibwet*, an unnatural snake viper, whose bite results in death. They also used poison (*ihyein*), which could result in *kwop* (leprosy) and could even lead to infertility. There were adequate checks and balances to control their excesses through *pa-ah* (sorcery) and administered punishment, according to tradition.

5.6 Religious Specialists

The principal religious ritual spiritualists in Tal were *Gu Kam Nwong, Gu Kam Mwandok, Gu Kam Na'an,* the chief-priest of Paikhok, and *Gu Kam Mangap.*

Gu Kam Nwong took care of *Nwong*, which came out at harvest for the protection of millet and guinea corn against theft.

Gu Kam Mwandok's major functional role was judgement and curtailing activities of wicked or evil people in the society.

Gu Kam Na'an's duties included initiation of children, ensuring peace and order and avoiding warfare.

The **chief-priest of Paikhok** handled administrative, political, socio-economic, health, and religious matters of the Tal community.

Gu Kam Mangap played a significant role over rain formation, respect for social organisations, and stratification as a cult group. Clan heads or chief-priests, who were believed to have supernatural powers, were very rare in the precolonial Tal community. Also, native doctors or herbalists were scarce. However, a few diviners were in existence. These diviners or healers were called *Gwimngu Kespa'ahmwa*. An example of such persons was Gugyei, at Kopzak. He used his powers to totally destroy all the evil spirits that were tormenting the people. He was a very powerful and popular person. Young, sharp, and intelligent persons were picked and groomed in secret for this privileged, recognised traditional role. They did not need to possess supernatural powers. Techniques used by the diviners include the following:

(i) *Pa'ah latu*: Consultations were made with the relevant stakeholders. After this, the diviner either placed the *latu* (small guard) on the ground or held it to him. Then the *latu* would start talking. An interpretation of the meaning of the talk was given simultaneously to the people concerned. The outcome or the result determined the nature of punishment or treatment to be administered.

(ii) *Pa'ah Phidah* (ventriloquism): A new calabash (*dah-damok*) was filled with water, and a type of special guinea corn (*matal*) was put in the water and stirred. As the diviner stirred the water, he would make some incantations. He would interpret the position and lining of the guinea corn to the parties concerned. Diviners did not prepare and administer the poison ordeal, rather they advised on who to contact, where to do it, or how the matter should be treated.

(iii) *Paah gap* was the last stage of investigation to find a solution when a critically sick person and relatives were involved.

There were herbalists who did not claim supernatural powers but were knowledgeable about medicinal herbs. For example, *Gwim Gu wa'at zem* were called to ward off snake venom and were traditional birth attendants. People with snake bites were treated by people with vast knowledge in the use of medicinal herbs. When bitten by a snake, an enemy was not allowed to pay a visit to the victim. After three days, it was known whether the patient would survive or not.

5.7 Delivery and Safety

To ensure a safe delivery, traditional birth attendants (men or women) would be available to apply either *kuul* or *phuk* and massage the pregnant woman if there was any difficulty. If that failed, a second attempt was made by rubbing *kuul* on her hand and inserting it into the vagina through the birth canal in order to remove the child by manipulation. This process was called *taah me'eh*. After delivery, the afterbirth (*guem*) was collected and disposed of. It was normally buried in an old small pot (*gugtul*) at the back of the house (*dangkhonglu*). Disposal of the afterbirth was done by a person chosen by the family.

5.8 After Delivery

As for the naming of children at birth, there were no ceremonies. Parents did not like the idea of naming children at an early stage, for fear of premature death. But the day the remains of the umbilical cord attached to the navel dropped, the child was commonly called according to gender (*nalem* for female and *dazhit* for male). A male child bore that name until a proper name was given to him after (circumcision (*sum vwang*). However, girls could be given a name after six months.

5.9   Initiation and Circumcision Ceremony.

When boys were five years old, they were circumcised. It was usually a community affair. Initial arrangement for circumcision took place at Paikhok; for example, Koptan and Tangge communities met and fixed a date for the occasion. When this had been done, relations of male children who were older than five were informed to prepare the children for the exercise by first shaving their hair completely. Based on this, villages such as Takhong, Mudong, Tangge, Hamtul, Mungkhot Kongkhol, Basnuang, and Kopzak would meet at a central place in their localities.

The ceremony began with two villages that played with each other, showing their mutual relationship by a special kind of greeting. For example, Hamtul and Kabwai people would recognise their play mates, they would call one another with nicknames or some kind of coded language, and they responded to one another. Similarly, these warm signs of relationship between villages were done by other communities.

Immediately after confirmation of the exercise, trumpets (*fier*) would be blown very loudly, marking the commencement of the initiation and circumcision exercise. The sound of trumpets was used as a cover to prevent the cries of children in pain from being heard. When it was finished, they would come out of the shrine, with only a few being circumcised as samples. Every locality group went back home to complete the process in their own shrine. If the circumcision was done incorrectly, and a child died as a result of sickness or infection, he was buried in the shrine. Relations of those who died were informed that during Dawen period, *Nwong* had taken the child (during *Na'ankhip* period, *Na'an* had taken it). Those circumcised had to stay in the shrine for three months (December-March) to ensure that the wounds were completely healed. If the wound was not completely healed, then the father took care of it at *Kapzang mai* (family shrine).

5.10 Burial

The rite of passage was common. In the preliminary stages, the death was announced as follows: After a person died, his uncle's people were the first to be notified. If they died in the morning, they would be informed immediately. But if it was in the evening, they would be told very early in the morning (by five o'clock). The notice was traditionally accompanied by a *guyeih* with a goat to make it official. Public announcement ("*Yong pe*") of the dead was done through the *Miskom Dil*.

The corpse was prepared by giving the body a special final bath. It was then dressed with the best attire, while his relations dug the grave at the community cemetery. If he was a devout traditional religious worshipper, his brothers would provide a big he-goat to be given to *Nwong* (tutelary genius) for offering as a sacrifice at the burial. However, if he was not rich, they would bring a big cock. The goat would be brought later. Thus, *Nwong* took centre stage. In the morning, between five and six o'clock, people, especially women, were not allowed to cry loudly before the burial. *Nwong* was the first to mourn *Maap* in the shrine. The corpse was dressed in traditional clothing, and the mourning was very colourful. People from his village and those around would come blowing trumpets, dancing in full warfare regalia, with bows, arrows, and shields. They would demonstrate how to fight in order to prevent opponents from removing grass from his thatched house, which was always the practice. Dancing and *Askuwet,* the mock warfare demonstration, continued up to ten o'clock in the morning for ordinary people and noon for *Dikum* (when "*Kum zum,*" tutelary genius, goes home) before they stopped and dispersed. Women then started a loud cry as soon as the corpse was taken out for burial at the cemetery.

The shape of the grave was circular, like that of a well. The corpse was buried in a sitting position (Meek, 1931). Rituals associated with internment include placing a spear in his right hand before the grave was closed. In others, the grave was covered before the spear was placed on the grave with an announcement by kinsmen (*Gupan*) telling God that so-and-so person was dead. The grave was covered with a big round stone; no soil or sand was pushed inside. The corpse was escorted to the grave with a female goat before it was returned to the house.

Subsequently, a kind of inquest (known as *kespaah*) was made into the cause of death. This is done when all the relations were gathered, together with the experts of *pa'ah*, about twelve in number. One of the twelve stirred the water, while the remaining eleven observed the process. The experts were selected from the different clans. This aspect was like a court in session, during which there was no noise, laughter or giggling, or sleeping. Only a red dress was worn. At the end of the day, the cause of the death was released by the experts to the relations. To ascertain whether the deceased was a witch or not, the skull was not removed. However, in most cases, the result of the investigation was not revealed. The experts were usually silent over such speculation or suspicion.

5.11 Ideas Concerning the Causes of Illness and Death

In traditional belief, the common causes of illness and death included the following:

(i)   leprosy (*Kwop*)
(ii) smallpox (*Ndwang*)
(iii) measles (*Hemlet*)
(iv) celebro-spinal meningitis (*Lam Thog* or *Tep Thog*)
(v)   witchcraft (*Tset*)

Explanation of the traditional beliefs concerning the causes of some of these illnesses was as follows:

Leprosy (*Kwop*): People believed that it was contracted through drinks as a result of poison. Some assert that it could be due to a mistake committed by the *Miskom Dil*, as a result of *Kum gu fok* (dirty tutelary genius) or fornication, or *Khyel*, a bad cancerous wound.

Measles and smallpox: It was believed that they were brought by wicked people or evil spirits. When someone died of an illness, such as smallpox as mentioned above, or snake bite, it was considered to be sufficient cause. It was believed that there must be a background or supernatural evil element that was responsible for the illness and eventual death of any member of the community.

5.12 The Ritual Year

Festivals in Tal were celebrated to mark the occurrence of particular events by occasional festivals. They were not necessarily tied to farming, rain rites, or first fruits.

Examples of these occasional festivals include the following:

(i)   *Na'anshang*
(ii) *Dideng (Tal blues)*
(iii) *Khung la Yang*
(iv) *Khung Dhai*

(v)   *Komting*

(vi)   *Tam shal*

(i)   ***Na'anshang*:** This was a traditional ceremony performed in the shrine during initiation and circumcision of young males from five years and above. It was not done in the open so as to avoid women and other underage children from watching what was going on. It was done after ten years as a celebration of thanksgiving to God, for bringing out the children successfully. However, there were two types. One was *Naan Dawen* and the other was *Na'ankhip*. They came out at intervals of five years, and *Na'an Dawen* was always the first to come. The division was due to the growing period of children after a five-year interval.

The process started with a discussion at Paikhok which involved fixing the date and commencement of circumcision ceremony. For Na'ankhip, it was Koptan that started while others followed as agreed upon in their locality's shrines.

In the middle of the circumcision period, about a month, all the children were taken out at once to the river very early in the morning; all women were warned to stay indoors (*suweb zumlu*). The leaders of the circumcision exercise always had their children (known as "*Gyep thim*") in front, and movement was in one single line.

Na'an Dawen also started with a discussion at Paikhok, and then others would go ahead and do theirs after a date had been fixed. Those at Basnuang did it with Kwaya interchangeably, while those at the shrine in the camp (*la thim,* Takhong) were always the first to be circumcised (that is, the children of *Dikum Kum*). They must start with them before other people's children. After one week, the children were taught how to blow the trumpet. "*Fier*", *khung gu tah* (how to beat big drum) part of initiation, "*askuwet*" warfare practice (fencing of any strong man with a stick as a defence). Tree climbing exercise was a kind of manhood or boyhood training. Food was served without salt for one month. Thereafter special protein-laden food was provided: chicken or bush meat.

For one month, every morning, all the children were taken for bathing in the river; all women were to stayed indoors so as not to see the children (*suweb zumlu*).

About a week before the exercise was over, the children were taken to the bush for another practice ("*Na'an segun npeni*"); a lot of beating and flogging took place, and trumpets were blown. Sharing took place in the shrine (*Ndong "yep"*) in the bush. Then, *honey* and *lhip* (a red powdered substance) were used to decorate their heads (*Lekhagu Kin Lhip*). This took place in the bush; bush meat was killed for the children, and by six o'clock, they were returned to the clan shrine. *Mat lap gigyepmwa* received the children from *Nwong*. Actually, *Nwong* would ask her how many children she gave out for the circumcision. It must be a woman who was intelligent and no longer giving birth or married. The exact number must be given. If there was a mistake, *Nwong* would take that child away from her. That night, new names would be given to all the children. The next day, *Dawen* dance ceremony continued, during which different foodstuff was given. For instance, food prepared from grains—millet and sorghum—were brought according to clans and family for two weeks. Whatever was brought was put in a bag and then emptied into a pot. Final ceremony, the millet and special meat, prepared with Beni seed, was given to make them brave.

(ii) **Dideng** was a kind of special dance (performing arts) for Tal blues, done mainly by young people (male and female). It was like a recreational dance in the evenings after a hard day's work. Sometimes, the dance took place in the evenings from six o'clock to midnight during moonlight. This was one of the most important aspects of Tal performing arts, because through it, friendship bonds and courtship leading to marriage proposals were made. Impressions of the boy's ability to perform were likely to touch the hearts of ladies, and a follow-up was usually made to sustain such relationships. It was a yearly event in September, after farm work was reduced.

(iii) **Khung La yang** took place after the general harvest period to say thank you to the gods for a year of good harvest and no ill health or war.

(iv) ***Khung Dhai*** was a ceremonial dance to mark the death of an elderly man, aged seventy and above. It was done as an expression of respect by the community for the departed elder, whose valuable contributions would be greatly missed, also to thank the gods for allowing him to live so long before his death.

(v) ***Komting*****:** This was done every ten years. It was a kind of dance that marked the demonstration of magical power by males and also to seek help to protect the community. Only seasoned men participated in the display.

(vi) ***Tam shal*****:** a ceremonial dance that occurred every ten years. The dance promoted the cementing of relationships among clans and was done only during the dry season as a kind of recreation. Farming activities were minimal; *Eighyet/Buut* was used for dancing.

Conclusion

The knowledge of a people's world-view is very crucial in understanding their socio economic, cultural, political, and even psychological problems. Evidence of this is demonstrated in the belief system of the Tal people, where almost all human activities were interpreted in the context of the rule of law and the relationship with Na'an, the supreme being in the universe. It was based on this that communal activities such as administration of justice, socio-political organisation, ceremonies, performing arts, and agriculture were carried out. To a large extent, most of this was practised as tradition by the Tal people. It is noteworthy that Christianity and other foreign religions have watered down some of the traditional practices.

References

Ames, C. G. (1934). *Gazetteer of the Plateau Province,* Vol. iv, Jos Native Administration. London: Frank Cass and Co. Ltd., p. 138.

Dikon, W. W. (1967). "Outline of Tal Culture." Unpublished Document.

Gabkwet, Andrew (2004). Informant from Kopzak interviewed on 03/02/2003 on the killing of Langkuk and evil spirits by Gugyei, a powerful leader. Age 56 years.

Guting, Kumwaih (2003). Informant in Tal intervieved on 16/06/2003 on the cosmology of Tal. Age 60-plus years.

Gwamna, J. D. (1996). *Gbagyi Names: Religious and Philosophical Connotations.* Nigeria: Gbagyi Visions Js, p. 5-6.

Meek, C. K. (1971). *The Northern Tribes of Nigeria.* London: Frank Cass and Co. Ltd. p. 12-33, 123, and 212.

Rumtong, Yakubu Mitok (2004): An informant interviewed on 08/03/2004 on Tal social organisation, trade and exchange, hunting, precolonial rule, and the killing of Langkuk in 1917. Age 90-plus.

Talya, Luka Lukding (2003). Informant interviewed on Tal, traditional religion on 08/03/2003 at Nakwan, in Shendam LGA. Age 53 years.

Tal Community Development Association (1988). Programme for Launching N500,000 development appeal fund. Nefur, Panskhin, Plateau State, Nigeria.

Chapter Six

The Killing of Langkuk in Tal

6.1 Coming of Colonial Rule and the Killing of Langkuk on Wednesday, 26 September 1917

Oral tradition posits that Europeans invaded the Hill tribes of Plateau, Tal inclusive, in the early 1900s (1902-1906). These tribes tried to resist the white man's rule but met with brutal force. The people of Tal were subdued because of the use of superior weapons, including machine guns. Resistance by any community or objection to organised labour always led to arbitrary arrests and detention. In fact, these detentions could last for a couple of months. However, sentences that were up to six months had to be officially passed by the colonial master.

According to oral tradition, the British came to Tal from Langtang through Vongrong (Takhong). The officer who came was led by the people to Kabwai and later on sent to Kopzak, where he was warmly accepted. He came in the company of some Ngas people (called *Pess* in Tal dialect). These Ngas men could speak Hausa language, and so they acted as interpreters to the white man. Thus, messages in English were interpreted into Hausa or Ngas, as the case may be, for the benefit of the white man and Tal people.

Langkuk was one of the Ngas people who used to accompany the white man to Tal. He was known to have travelled very widely, covering places such as Bauchi, Zaria, Sokoto, and Kano (before its invasion in 1893). His close association with Hausa traders enabled him to learn and become very fluent in the language and also conversant with the system of traditional administration. Given this exposure, he was picked as one of the interpreters and carriers of the white man. Langkuk became popular as he kept following the colonial masters on tours. Having established a good rapport, he became the mouthpiece of the white man. Messages relayed by him were considered true and reliable, as good as if they were coming from the white man.

Over the years at different occasions, messages continued to come through Langkuk, asking the people to bring various food items such as eggs, yam, groundnuts, corn flour, and livestock (goats, sheep, and cattle, *Ning Tal, Muturu,* traditional short-horned cattle). Responses to most of these requests were promptly made by Tal people. These food items were eventually collected at certain intervals. The people took these items to Pankshin on foot from Tal and had to spend a week before coming back home to Tal.

Colonial rule came with the introduction of forced labour. So even before the appointment of a divisional officer (1910-1915), forced labour became very severe.

Tal people became suspicious of frequent visits and the demand of Langkuk and his men's use of force to grab anything they could lay their hands on. Besides, they were taken aback with the doubling of the number of members of his entourage, who assisted in collecting whatever was seen as being good through forceful acquisition for Langkuk.

In 1915, Langkuk set out on tour as the team leader to areas such as Kabwir, Amper, Ampang-East, Pai, Tal, Garram, Chip, Mangu, and Bokkos. Upon arrival at Tal, they were warmly received by the chief of Tal and leaders of the people. Langkuk, who had been acting as an interpreter in the previous years, assumed a leadership position. He became a black white man, dishing out orders to followers to do whatever pleased him, which the white men never did. What is interesting is the postulation that the early years of protectorate government combined Tal and other people in one administration under the chief of Pankshin. This was a mistaken endeavour, which no doubt the government would not have countenanced had they possessed a fuller knowledge of the people. Tal resented it, and the chief of Pankshin (Langkuk) ventured to make a ceremonial visit to Tal with a retinue of followers (Ames, 1934, p. 49).

6.2 Appointment of Langkuk as the Third Chief of Pankshin (Ner) 24 September 1917 as Fourth Class Chief

Lankuk was one of the Ngas people that the the British looked for, a strong man through whom to rule as, the chief of Pankshin.

Having appointed Langkuk as leader, the British colonial masters steadily extended his jurisdiction, and he committed many atrocities during World War I. For instance, he imposed a tax with extra forced labour, and members of his entourage seized anything good to their eyes. This was an abnormal practice, because the white man did not behave like that before. Besides, why did he come in company of so many people, including women? Their plundering activities became highly suspicious by the people of Tal, who concluded that he was not sent by the white man. If Langkuk was actually representing the white man's interest, Tal people wondered why their wives and daughters were not spared. Women were forcefully taken away from their husbands, and unmarried girls were forced into marriage without their consent and taken to Pankshin. His behaviour was unworthy because women and girls who refused to submit were severely tortured. Their hands and legs were tied apart, exposing their vagina in public and putting in millet or guinea corn, then driving chicken or ducks to peck and feed on it. This was a very painful and dehumanising experience for the women and girls. Also, pepper was applied in some cases, as confirmed by Usnna from Belning, who came back and later remarried a man called Dokle.

The young men were not spared either. They had to head-load the entire foodstuffs collected, including livestock like cattle, to Pankshin and never returned.

Foodstuffs that were carried to Pankshin were directed to be kept in dark rooms in Ner, where people were either trapped or pushed into deep pits or holes. To escape being trapped and not come back as others, the young men had to bind themselves in a line with the hand of their *bente* (*Thun*) being tied together. So if any of them was pushed, they noticed it quickly and pulled back. This precautionary measure kept them from escaping.

His administration was regarded as a reign of terror. For instance, in one episode, sixteen young and strong men were ordered by Langkuk to carry a live shorthorn cow (*Muturu* in Hausa or Ning-Tal) to Pankshin. The young men obeyed for fear of being maltreated and carried the bull on a stretcher and put it on their heads. The bull was carried as ordered, as their lives were in danger. The young men were able to reach Tat-Chik in Kwashi-Ungwan Galadima, about eight kilometres from Kwopzak. However, the young men got tired and could not go further, so they were instructed to slaughter the bull. This action was taken in consultation with Langkuk, through Yete, one of his bodyguards. The meat was carried to Pankshin, a distance of about fifty miles, by eight strong young men. None of them ever came back. The rock and place upon which the bull was slaughtered is called *Tat-Chik* ("sharpened knife" in the Tal language) in remembrance of that barbaric act (see figure 6.1).

Figure 6.1. Tat-Chik

People had a lot of grudges against Langkuk. What disturbed them very much was the fact that the men who conveyed all the various items to Pankshin never came back. The question was, "What happened to them?" Among the women who were abducted or forcefully taken away, only one returned. What happened to the rest? Were they sold into slavery to Hausa traders or were they killed? Some people even speculated that they became part of the Ner people. In fact, before his last visit to Tal, there were widespread rumours that the men were used as a sacrifice to the gods. These rumours later on became true as two of the people who were taken away confirmed it. These surviving eyewitnesses were Usnna, who later came back to Belning, and Nafwen, who later came back to Da'an and died in 1963

6.3 Langkuk's Last Visit to Tal and Why He Was Killed

An atmosphere of outrage was already brewing high among the people of Tal because of the atrocities of Langkuk. He was warned by the British to be careful and not to collect anything in excess, but he refused to heed to their advice. He had great faith in his charms. It should be noted that several attempts were made to kill Langkuk by other tribes. For example, he was attacked near Dok in Pe, in June 1917. He narrowly escaped with his life, but seven of his followers were killed and thirteen wounded (Colonial report SN/PIO/S14711P/1917). He was regarded as a terror all over Pankshin Division and not particularly by one tribe alone; as a result, all the tribes made plans to eliminate him.

In September 1917, another visit to Tal was planned by Langkuk and his collaborators. Meanwhile, the people of Tal received the information with mixed feelings because previous visits were not actually on the white man's order. Furthermore, it was confirmed that most of the foodstuff and other items collected at Tal were distributed among his kiths and kindred. To crown it all, it was confirmed that the men and women who had been forcefully abducted and taken to Pankshin were not alive. They were never seen again, and nobody ever heard about them, nor were they seen as part of his entourage.

Langkuk arrived in Kopzak from Pe on 25 September 1917, when Mutkhai Ranme was the chief of Tal. He came in the company of a very large number of people, numbering up to fifty-two. This gave the Tal people an impression that he did not mean well and suspected that he was out on another mission of looting and plundering of their farm products.

On Wednesday, 26 September 1917, on Balong market day, Langkuk asked Mutkhai to get him some strong men to take to Pankshin, but Rumbok (brother to Mutkhai) disagreed. His refusal was based on the ground that his son Fotgwim had not come back from Pankshin. He was quite sad and something had to be done. The line of action—capital punishment—was secretly revealed only to Takhong, Wetal, and Kabyak. The chief refused to cooperate, saying that such a thing should not happen during his time or on his land. There was tension and an uproar when the elders and chiefs were informed about the visit. They doubted that the food items collected, such as pumpkin (*biyap*) and cocoyam (*gwan*), were actually eaten by the white man. Mutkhai was subjected to interrogation and asked many questions, which he could not readily provide answers. These were the principal questions:

i.   Where are the eight men who carried the cow meat (*Muturu*) that was slaughtered at Tat-Chik to Pankshin?

ii.   Where are the other men who carried foodstuff and eggs for the white man to Pankshin?

iii.   Are all these men in his entourage?

iv.   Where are our wives and daughters who were forcefully abducted and taken away from us to Pankshin?

v.   How long will these looting expeditions by Langkuk continue in the name of the white man?

vi.   The white man came here and proclaimed peace, so when has he become a looter and man-eater? When he came, our young men escorted him and carried his loads to Pankshin and came back after one week. But what happened to those who escorted Langkuk for the past two years now? None came back. Tell us where these men and women are (Gabkwet, 2004).

Mutkhai told the congregation that he could not provide answers but they should reserve the questions for Langkuk to answer. Dissatisfied with his response, the elders and chiefs sought a way to avoid another calamity or ruthless treatment of their people. Warriors of valour and men with magical powers were put on red alert. Several consultative meetings were held and it was resolved that unless their men and women were part of the entourage, the entire retinue of Langkuk were to be captured. The chief (Mutkhai) was very reluctant and not in support of the plan to kill Langkuk, but he had no option. The elders told him whether he was in support or not, it must be carried out. If he tried to thwart their effort, he would be joined up as a victim. In the long run, he succumbed, probably because there was speculation that he connived with Langkuk to execute that barbaric behaviour.

All necessary arrangements were made pending his arrival from Pe. There were two options:

i. If the men were seen in his entourage, no action will be taken against him.
ii. If the men and women were not seen, then all of them, including Langkuk and others, should be placed under arrest for questioning. Where there was no convincing or satisfactory answer concerning these Tal men and women, severe action will be taken against Langkuk and his collaborators.

The young men and women became panicky when the news of Langkuk's arrival was received in Tal. Ladies or girls of marriage age were told to stay indoors. He stayed in the house of Mutkhai, who might have discussed the demand of his people with him. Langkuk thought it was going to be business as usual, but it was not to be. For instance, he had earlier told Mutkhai that he should get some strongmen for him to take to Pankshin. So in the morning of 26 September 1917, Rumbok came and Langkuk was told that one of the men he had asked for had come. He ordered his arrest, but Rumbok shouted for help and said that Langkuk should be arrested. Langkuk saw men that lay siege but still had confidence in his charms.

Langkuk was captured with his entire entourage. The man who ordered the arrest of Langkuk and fifty-two people was Gabkwet. He was asked to account for the whereabouts of the men and women he took to Ner, in Pankshin. At first he said that they were not killed but were still alive. However, on further interrogation, he confessed that they were all killed except some women, who were still alive. Dissatisfied and angry with his oscillating answer, he was kept separately in a shrine because of his magical powers. It would be recalled that attempts had been made on the life of Langkuk in several other places but to no avail. It was believed that once his blood came in contact with the soil, he would reincarnate. Based on that belief, he was tied up and dropped into a very large pot (*Palang*) full of boiling water to ensure that his blood was never spilled.

In retaliation for the loss of their men and women, Langkuk and his followers were killed on 26 September 1917. Langkuk tried to escape using his magical powers by changing or incarnating into dragon fly or rat, lizard, cockroach, or gecko, but he was subdued by superior powers.

The principal actors responsible for the killing were renowned warriors, namely Miskom Gabkwet Bamkop Malong (the person who was instrumental in the arrest of Langkuk), Miskom Rumbok, Ranme, and Gubum Dilma. Another view has it that Bakkhung from Kyam and Bakkuk from Wetal participated in the act. Langkuk would have been declared missing in transit were it not for one Khopkwelep (a man from Amper, one of his followers), who escaped on horseback to Pankshin and reported the incident. He met a woman in the bush, and she revealed to him that something had happened, and that is how he was able to escape.

6.4 Terrible Aftermath of the Killing of Langkuk and Fifty-Two Others

News of the outrage was reported by the escapee (Khopkwelep) to the colonial officer in Pankshin. The information was immediately relayed to the headquarters in Jos, the seat of the colonial administration at Naraguta.

The Tal people were terrorised and traumatised by the wanton destruction of life and property. Mutkhai, the district head of Tal who was appointed by the colonial masters, disappeared for three days into Muri province (Taraba plains). But some people believed that he was driven out of Tal because he played host to Langkuk. However, he was later arrested, detained, and taken to Pankshin, where he died in detention. Mutkhai was punished and held responsible for allowing the killing of Langkuk and others.

Soldiers of World War I (1914) stationed at Bukuru were drafted to Pankshin with authorisation of the governor general. They arrived Pankshin in October 1917. The contingent that arrived included Lieutenant F. H. Bush (commanding patrol officer), Lieutenant Micholson (a British non-commissioned officer), Dr McLory (the medical officer, later relieved by Dr Wood), two subalterns, 102 rank-and-file foot soldiers, and seven policemen.

The following fighting equipment was mobilised for the operation in Tal:

i. Seven machine guns (see figure 6.2) ii. Nine boxes of ammunition and other loads (Residents of Bauchi Province, 1916)

Figure 6.2. Machine gun (similar to the type used in 1917)

Their mission was to bring the outrage under control and the ringleaders to account for what happened and also to establish the cause of the rebellion.

Operations commenced in Tal on 21 October and lasted to 4 December 1917. Forty-six days were engaged in hostilities. A large force was used because the field commanders feared that Tal people could mobilise and put their full fighting force of three thousand men into action (Micholson, 1917). This was confirmed in the military route report of John Molynoux (1917); see figure 6.3. He said that thirty policemen were inadequate to face Tal's standing army of three thousand men. He recommended the use of West African Frontier Force (WAFF).

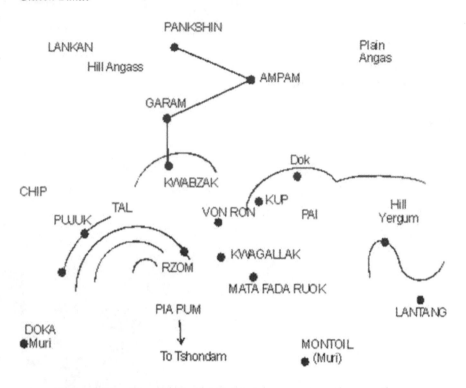

PANKSHIN

LANKAN   Plain
                                                     Angas
    Hill Angass

                              AMPAM

GARAM

                              Dok

CHIP   KWABZAK

          TAL   KUP   Hill
  PUJUK   VON RON   PAI   Yergum

                    KWAGALLAK

              RZOM

              MATA FADA RUOK

       PIA PUM   LANTANG

DOKA
●Muri   MONTOIL
          To Tshondam   ● (Muri)

Tal could possibly put in the field 3,000 fighting men - in Molynoux's
opinion 30 police are quite inadequate to deal with the situation - and
suggests that a company of West African Frontier Force (WAFF).

Source: John H. Molynoux, 1917

Figure 6.3. Routes of Colonial Military Operations in Tal, 1917

The soldiers in company of the Pankshin people came looting and shooting indiscriminately. Standing crops were cut down, and houses were burnt to ashes. The presence of the army and their militant posture did not intimidate them. In any case, most of them were already evacuated to safety in the hills. The terrain was very difficult for troop movement or access. In response to the order given to the Tal people by the soldiers to surrender the actors, the Tal people replied by telling the soldiers to come up the hills and collect the ringleaders if they were truly men.

Establishing a truce was not easy. Several messengers were sent to appeal to the Tal people to submit or come in for dialogue on the matter, but they were turned down. However, in November 1917, Rumbok, one of the ringleaders, was handed over to them. With this development, orders were given to the commanding officer to cease all movement of troops. A truce was eventually established on 29 November 1917. Village headmen came and informed the divisional officer that they refused to have Mutkhai back as their chief and that they had elected Fotgwim, son of Rumbok, in his place. They told the commanding officer the reason for their action. Rumbok and others who were the ringleaders accepted responsibility and were ready to face the consequences. From the date of the truce, several parties voluntarily came in and out of the colonial military camp without fear. The people had returned to their houses and brought abundant food supplies for them. The Pankshin-Tal operation ended with the movement of troops from Tal to Chip on 5 December 1917; they arrived in Panksin the next day (Cote, 1918a).

The colonial records of 1918 indicate that seventy natives (or "pagans") were killed and one soldier (carrier) was wounded. The details are shown in table 6.1.

Table 6.1: Consequences of Colonial Military Patrol in Tal in 1917

S/No	Date	Location	Nature of Attack/ Consequences
1	22/10/1917	Vongrong, Kwaklak	Police open fire, 1 pagan killed
2	22/10/1917	Amtoul (Hamtul)	Officer Commanding Operations, 14 pagans killed
3	23/10/1917	Men of Hamtul and Basniong (Basnuang) in pursuit of Fotgwim	Officer in Charge search surrounding bushes, destroyed war camps, houses, and beer crops (millet and guinea corn) of the chief men implicated
4	23/10/1917	Near Hamtul	Two people killed
5	25/10/1917	Near Basniong (Basnuang)	Seven killed, recovery of large property alleged to belong to late Langkuk and his members

S/No	Date	Location	Nature of Attack/ Consequences
6	26/10/1917	Kyam	Police opened fire, 2 people killed
7	26/10/1917	Hamtul	Commanding Officer opened fire and killed 2 persons
8	27/10/1917	Tal-Buzuk	Col. Faulkes attacked while returning from Ibi zone in hot pursuit of assailants; found 11 dead bodies
9	27/10/1917	Garam-Kwopzak Road	Travellers attacked by Tal men, in response colonial soldiers cut down all crops along the road
10	28/10/1917	Medong (Mudong)	Opposition encountered, counterattack by soldiers; 11 casualties were recorded
11	29/10/1917	Near Medong (Mudong)	Escort of 2 women found near Kwaklak to Mudong by soldiers; five shots were fired and 3 people were killed
12	2/11/1917	Mudong	Return visit attack, police fired 5 rounds Killed 1 person but several large bodies were collected near Mudong; later on police fired 3 rounds, killing 5 people.
13	3/11/1917	Near Vongrong (Takhong)	An officer encountered attack, fired back, and 8 people were killed and properties of Langkuk were found

Source: Colonial Records of 1917, Panshin Native Authority and Residents of Bauchi Province reports to the Secretary, Northern Provinces, Kaduna, 15 April 1918.

References

Benue Plateau Government (1973). Nigerian Population Census: Important Historical and Local Events, Pankshin Division. pp. 14-15.

Cote, F. G. Health (1917). Progress Report; Pankshin Tal Patrol. Henry Bush Lieutenant (1917) confidential letter to Captain Headquarters Nigerian Regt., Officer Commanding. Final Report, Pankshin Patrol Tal military.

Cote, F. G., Health (1918a). Assistant District Officer (A.D.0.) Letter to the District Officer; 6th Progress Report, Pankshin Patrol, Naraguta Patrol Escorts.

Cote F. G., Health (1918b). Patrol Report; Sarkin Pankshin and fifty-two others killed by men of Tal. Colonial records. Ref no. SN/P10/S1471P/1917.

Gabkwet, Andrew (CSP Rtd.) (2004). Informant from Kwopzak (Tal royal house) interviewed on 26/06/2009 on why Langkuk was killed. Aged 56 years.

Longa, Adamu (2003). Informant interviewed on 08/02/2003 on the coming of colonial rule and killing of Langkuk. Aged 90 years; a migrant based in Nakwan, Shendam LGA. He is from Vongrong (Takhong) in Tal.

Malynoux, John H. (1917). Colonial Records. Reports of routes military operations in Tal. Ref no. SNPI015/471P/1917 Sarkin Pankshin and thirty others killed by men of Tal, military patrol.

Pike, R. N. (1913). Letter to the resident in charge, Naraguta Division, Ref No. SP/10/1/194P/1913 Central Province, Pankshin Disturbances, Yergam, Pe, and Thal. p. 4.

Residents of Bauchi Province (1918). Letter to Secretary, Northern Province, Kaduna Military Pankshin-Tal.

Chapter Seven

Colonial Rule in Tal

7.1   The Creation of Districts and Selection of District Heads

According to oral tradition, the creation of districts was based on dialogue. The geographical demarcation of land area occupied by different ethnic groups was done in consultation with the various stakeholders in the presence of the British colonial administrative officers. When a consensus was reached, mapping for official recognition and gazetting was then carried out, to indicate the exact boundaries of the districts. Every area in the present Pankshin and Kanke Local Government Areas existed as a kingdom until they were turned to sub-Native Authorities (NAs)

7.2   Origin of Chieftaincy and Selection Method

Tal consisted of twenty-two villages or hamlets with independent leadership (or headships). However, for administrative convenience, the colonial masters decided to establish or create the position of one stool through a white man who came from Langtang to Vongrong (Takhong). He was brought to Kabwai but uncertain of what to do; they took him to Kwopzak, where he was welcomed by the people. This gesture pleased him and so he ordered that a seat for a chief should be created to rule over the other groups in Tal. In principle, it marked the emergence of a ruling house. It is pertinent to note that it was not exclusive; others were involved, as evident by a letter dated 26 September 1945 and signed by the Divisional Officer (D.O.) Ref. Letter No. 81/63, Tal, and Pankshin Division. This communication emanated when the stool became vacant after the death of Bedung.

The divisional officer was directed to come to Tal and conduct an election in order to select a new chief. When he came, a meeting was held with all twenty-two elders of the entire Tal District. All representatives were present (except seven, who were absent). Three were very small villages or hamlets consisting of a few compounds, and four of medium size. Based on this fact, at least 80 percent of the elders were present at the meeting (District Officer, 1945).

Supervision of the exercise involved an in-depth discussion, consultation, and understanding of the traditions and local customs governing the choice of a head chief, which were meticulously followed. According to the tradition, the *Gwollong Kum* (chief-priest) usually nominated a candidate for the post of district head (*Gwollong Tal*), in consultation with all twenty-two elders. Selection process was by rotation (*Tungdeh*). Following the traditional due process, *Gwollong Kum* at that time was Nyimes, who said he nominated Lafuk. However, *Nyimwes* is not the name of a person but the leaf of the locust bean tree; it was used as a final process of confirming an elected chief. The divisional officer acknowledged the nomination of a candidate to succeed Bedung. Therefore, he called all twenty-two elders of the different units of Tal and asked each one in turn to say who they wanted. With one exception, they all supported Lafuk. The person who objected was Gubis, as shown in the genealogical tree, who wanted to be made the chief but had not even a single backer. So he was disregarded. Thus, the general consensus and decision was unanimously in favour of Lafuk. Given the development mentioned above, Lafuk was pronounced as the new chief (*Gollong Tal*). Locust bean tree leaves (*nyimmwes*) were immediately collected and put straight into Lafuk's *Bente* or *Thun* (triangular pant), signifying that he was traditionally installed at Fyangshik. This same method of traditional installation was practised by the Tal people in Tangale area in Gombe State, Nigeria.

Apart from the traditional procedure, consideration was also given to qualifying criteria. Official guidelines regarding the selection and eventual installation of a chief that were considered include the following:

i.   Official recognition of the name as a clan leader as reflected in the genealogical tree of Tal chiefs.
ii.   He should be mature (age fifty years and above) but should also command respect.
iii.   He should have a high status; for instance, Lafuk was a salaried member of Tal Native Court for a long time.

iv. General qualifications for the post: he must be a man of substance and richly endowed. For example, Lafuk owned two large farms, three horses, five dwarf cows, *Muturu* (short horn cattle), two Fulani type of cattle, thirty goats, forty-five sheep, several *Itili* olive trees (*canarium swein furtii, ting pa'at* in the Tal language), and silk cotton trees.

Lafuk stood out because of his long-standing membership on the court; he was conversant with all local habits and Tal customs and could mobilise and unite the people.

In addition to the above, there were other qualifying criteria:

1. The man must be a village or hamlet head (*Mai angwa*).
2. He must enjoy good health and a sound mind.
3. He must never have been charged with any criminal offence before any court and be a good person (*Gwim gudeme*).
4. He must be literate; this was the only point which Lafuk did not possess, as he was illiterate. However, the main point in his favour was that all the elders were in support of his candidature to become the next chief of Tal.

Having completed the process of selection based on the official criteria and traditional guidelines, the result was forwarded to the secretary of the Northern Provinces in Kaduna, through the provincial officer in Jos, for confirmation as the district chief of Tal. See figure 7.1 for a genealogical tree of the chiefs of Tal.

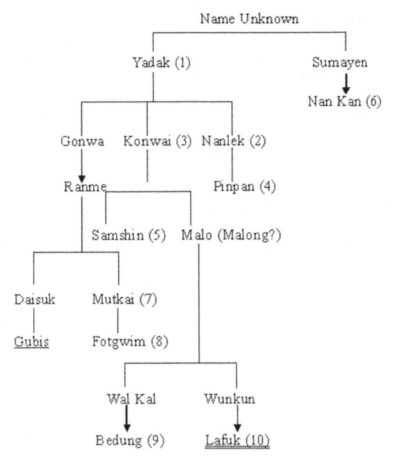

Source: Divisional Officer Pankshin Colonial Records 1945.

Figure 7.1: Genealogical tree of the chiefs of Tal

The genealogical tree above indicates the following:

1. Yadak is the first of the chiefs of Tal, as far as it is known today.
2. Chiefs from Yadak onwards are numbered in order of bearing office.
3. Bedung, who died in July 1945, is marked no. 9.
4. Gubis, who laid claim to the office, is underlined once.
5. Lafuk, the chosen successor, is underlined twice.

7.3 Functions of District Heads (Chiefs)

The main functions of district heads (chiefs) were tax collection and administration of justice among disputing persons or groups. Mobilisation of labour for public work was also part of their expected role. Taxation was in form of levies to be paid as tribute(s) by adults males in the district. It was collected centrally, for onward submission at the headquarters of the Pankshin Divisional Office. Payment was with crops produced by the farmers: guinea corn and millet (one bundle each), one goat, and a bundle of grass for thatching. The collection of all the items was called *"Dungku."* Anybody who failed to pay had his land confiscated or seized. Thus, people earned their tax by working hard to raise animals, produce food crops, make use of their labour, and cut and collect bundles of grass to meet their obligations. The idea of selling their labour was normal; everybody was proud to be known for working hard and paying their taxes when due. Taxes were also paid with cowries (*hasnamwet*) obtained along river systems. People who did not possess cowries had to give part of their land in exchange, sell it, or trade by barter with chickens, goats, or sheep in order to pay their annual tribute to the chief or colonial masters.

European currency was later on introduced. For instance, it was reduced to six pence per male adult (Pike, 1913). Collecting taxes was not an easy task and was resisted by the Tal people. Personal involvement of the British officers led to excessive abuse of power. For instance, in 1913, at Vongrong (Takhong), people refused to pay the tax and took up arms to fight, but the colonial officer, A. N. Pike, ordered the British Army's commanding officer to take charge, and operations commenced. Because of the use of superior weapons of the colonial army, the people retreated towards the bush between Pe and Tal, some breaking away near D. Mata, Fada, going into Muri Province. The pagan casualties were estimated at thirty-three killed. A great number of the casualties occurred when they made a final stand to prevent their stock from being driven off into Muri.

Abuses in the tax collection system were terrible. Excessive use of power resulted in loss of lives and property. For instance, at Kwopzak, some portion of the village was destroyed. Stock was collected to realise the Vongrong tax. This act was irrational. A much more diplomatic approach could have been used. Tax assessment methods were actually arbitrary.

7.4 Forced Labour

People were organised through imposition of compulsory participation in community development projects. Work was shared according to clans in order to promote competition and speedy completion of the projects at hand. Forced labour was introduced for the construction of schools, a dispensary, and roads. Attendance and participation was compulsory. For example, anyone who failed to come for road construction was made to pay a fine of one goat or four shillings (or more). Flogging was even used to ensure strict compliance. Disobedience and nonpayment of fines resulted in imprisonment. Thus, the schools and dispensary in Tal were built through organised forced labour. Under strict supervision, the dispensary was built in one month around 1936.

7.5 Creation of Native Courts

Administration of justice was managed by the district head and elders, who adopted trial by ordeal. Accused persons were subjected to all kinds of inhuman treatment or humiliating experiences. However, with the coming of the colonial masters and the establishment of Native Courts, trial by ordeal was abolished.

The Native Authority of Tal had a native court created, with the chief of Tal as the president, assisted by traditional advisers (elders: heads of twenty-two villages or hamlets) and Sarkin Hausawa Ibrahim (Pembleton, 1940). People selected as judges were usually men of wisdom and a sound mind, who were articulate and well respected. They were taken mainly from Kyam, Takhong, and Yong.

Patronage of the new courts was not very high because of arbitrary dispensation of justice. They were not quite impartial in arriving at decisions. Besides, fines were forcefully enforced. Thus, justice was not done, as treatment of cases were handled in such a manner, that the guilty parties sometimes got away with it. The redress sought by the aggrieved persons was never achieved. However, the chiefs did try to settle cases to date.

7.6 Colonial Administration of Pankshin Division and Formalisation of the Stool of Ngollong Ngas in 1978

The desire of the colonial masters was to have one paramount ruler in Pankshin Division for administrative convenience. This happened when Mangu was still a district in Pankshin Division. The idea was introduced when twelve Ngas-speaking districts decided to put their heads together to consider the idea of selecting one person among themselves. The district heads agreed, Mangu inclusive, and the person who emerged as the winner came from Mangu. The Ngas people, especially the chiefs, did not like it; they felt aggrieved and rejected the Mangu man, on the ground that he was an outsider (non-Ngas speaking). That was why they fashioned out a new idea, and together they came out with an agreement that only the twelve district heads should vote and only one person would be elected. The stool would rotate only among these districts, and this has continued to date.

The position was formalised by the Plateau State Government in 1978 (Plateau State of Nigeria Gazette, 1978). In that document, Section 3 states that "all district heads in the twelve districts of the local government shall be eligible as candidates for the election of the chieftaincy." The gazette was signed by Kasimu Idris, Secretary to the Military Government.

7.7 The Advent of Christianity in Tal

According to oral tradition, the first missionaries who came to Tal around the nineteenth century were from the Faith Tabernacle. The Faith Tabernacle of Nigeria brought Pastor Ezekiel, an Igbo man from Jos, before 1926. They came as traders or businessmen during the reign of Chief Bedung and later on established a church. Pastor Ezekiel came to trade, especially in groundnuts, but he also taught others and sponsored some in schools, including Yadil Dangway (Ayo Emmanuel Dangway's Father), Mutshell, and Gudil (who later died in school at Bukuru as a result of chicken pox).

The first converts were Bongliht and Yalep from Hamtul. Other prominent members included Gufwel from Dasuk, Mark Gudet Dembwep, Yadil Dangway and James Tuta Yieduwai from Hamtul, and Gunung from Kwopzak. Afterwards, Mr Amila and his wife, Mrs Mary Yarinye Amila, came from Nyalang in Pankshin District and joined them as members. Mr Amila was posted to work as a dispensary assistant.

The second group of missionaries that came to Tal were Roman Catholics from Shendam. This group established a church and a primary school at Kongnaan. Students of this school proceeded to Shendam to further their education.

A third group that came was the Sudan United Mission (SUM) from Kabwir. The group was led by Mr Barock, a white missionary. They established a church, and children of members went to Kabwir for primary school and then to Higher Elementary Teachers College, later renamed Gindiri Teachers College (now COCIN Comprehensive College, Gindiri). Boys Secondary School (BSS) and Girls High School (GHS) were at Gindiri, located in Mangu.

All three groups had places where they first settled. For example, Faith Tabernacle established their camp at Balong, which was (and is still) the district headquarters; they later moved to Ningnat. The Roman Catholic mission settled at Kongnan, and the Sudan United Mission established their base at Dunsung but later moved to Lawuya (now COCIN church). It is important to note that activities of Faith Tabernacle did not last, as they were unable to sustain their missionaries; most of the converts joined the SUM. Prominent among them were James Tuta Yeiduwai and Mark Gudet Dembwep.

7.8 Convertees and Life Experiences

There was a conflict of interest in some family homes because of the Christian faith professed by the children. For example, Litgwim was furious over the conversion of his daughter Nachik Litgwim, and so she had to take refuge with Gwaiwul Yohana in Dunyel. All manners of threats to life or deprivation from food were issued, but it was tactfully managed in such a way that this did not lead to loss of life. A major area of conflict was that Christian women could move freely, which was against the laws of traditional religion (idol worship) that restricted or prohibited their movement, especially when tutelary geniuses were out. The situation was so bad that Chief Bedung had to intervene in order to put an end to the practice in support of Christianity. According to him, Christians were his eyes or watch dogs. Thus, he did not want them to be molested during his regime.

7.9 Participation of Tal People in World War I and World War II

Contact with the outside world during the colonial era brought information about World War I and II to the area. These events attracted some Tal men, who volunteered and enlisted and fought in the world wars. The following men participated in World War I:

1. Audu Shiktal (Buzuk)
2. Laran (Dasuk)
3. Datyiem (Buzuk)
4. Ahmadu Kyepkong
5. Pangrat (Dan)
6. Audu Kwaldun (Kyam)
7. Yaro Zwangnan (Kabwai)
8. Sabo Pankshin (Guyin Yatep) from Kabwai

Sabo Pankshin was one of those who fought in World War I and World War II. According to him, veterans of World War II included the following:

1. Sabo Pankshin (had British rank of sergeant up to retirement; see figure 7.2)
2. Sabo Gyebzim (Kwopzak)
3. Inusa Mutlong (Kabwai)
4. Ali Degweh (Kwopzak)
5. Adu Kwaldun
6. Sambo Gutip (Kabwai)
7. Naankhin Gwetdut (Kopgol)
8. Mangna (Young)
9. Pestuwa (Kabyak)
10. Audu Pebwap (Tangge)
11. Kantoma Gubing (Kwopzak/Pangya)
12. Lagutitit (Kwopzak)
13. Garba Gukwet (Munkhort/Kabwai)
14. Audu Lamunkhort

15. Naanlong Takhong (Burma War, India)
16. Ditmwa Takhong
17. Gutam Tanko Tangge (Dr Yohana Tanko's father)
18. Audu Naanhei (Tangge)
19. Sabo Kopluk (Tangge)
20. Sabo Gupat (Kabyak)
21. Khisgwim (Kyam), a brother to Zemdang; all were at Burma War and India
22. Zemdang (Kyam)
23. Sabo Kankuk (Kwaklak) (he was in 9 Batallion, known to be very troublesome; bullets never got him)
24. Adamu Gutus Mutkhai (Kwopzak) (enlisted in the army but did not participate or go to the war front because it had already ended)
25. Saidu (Young)

World War II brought direct employment to all the young, able, strong, energetic men who enlisted into the army. It opened up room for development in Tal. For instance, people then saw the need to go to school and go to the markets to buy clothes; ideas about sanitation and cleaning their compounds daily were introduced. This led to the building of a dispensary for health care delivery services and improved agricultural production to uplift their economic status.

Also, the excesses of the chiefs of Tal were checkmated by the returning war veterans. They were challenged openly, without fear. For example, when Pangrat, one of the veterans, heard that Chief Bedung took his fiancée by force, he took his gun and headed straight to the palace. On getting there, he shot into the air, and this created pandemonium. People started running, and Chief Bedung came out to ask what was the matter. Pangrat demanded that his future wife be released immediately. Upon hearing this, Bedung was disturbed and, for fear of any unpleasant consequences, had no option than to comply. He quickly brought out the girl. Pangrat then took her to his house.

Although the war opened up opportunities for development, it also caused social nuisance in society. For instance, seizure of property by force was a common practice by some war veterans.

111

Figure 7.2: Sabo Guyin Yatep, a World War II veteran interviewed on October 14, 2011, in Shendam LGA, Plateau State, Nigeria.

References

Dangway, E. D. (2003). Informant interviewed on 08/03/2003 on colonial rule and impact of World War II on Tal. Age 82 years.

Pankshin, S. G. Yatep (2011). WWI and WWII veteran interviewed on 14/10/2011, Shendam. Aged 75-plus years.

Pembleton, E. S., Resident Plateau (1940). Colonial Records Jos, Profile Ref. No. 1/1/3639, Tal District, Pankshin Division 1940. p. 45.

Pike, R. N. (1913). Letter to the Resident in Charge, Naraguta Division. Assistant Resident Archival Records File No. SP/10/1/194P/1913, Central Province, Pankshin Disturbances, yergam, Pe, and Thal. Naraguta Division, Jos. p. 4.

Plateau State of Nigeria Gazette (1978). The Chief's Appointment and Deposition Law (CAP. 20) (Appointment of Chief of Angas) Order, 1978 Gazette No. 15, Vol. 13, 4, May, supplement part B.

Rumtong, Mitok Yakubu (2004). Informant interviewed on 26/03/2004 on colonial rule in Tal Age 90-plus years.

Chapter Eight

Colonial Attack 1917 and Migration to the Plains

The word "migration" means "movement under natural forces" (Oxford Dictionary of Current English, 2001, p. 562). However, the movement of Tal people to the lowland plains in Shendam was not largely due to the influence of natural forces. It was man-made, because many people left as a result of colonial conquest. Intimidated by the soldiers of the colonial masters during the outrage about the killing of Lankuk and the high-handedness of some of the chiefs, the people left Tal and went to Shendam.

8.1 The Reasons for the Migration to the Plains

The push factors responsible for the migration of Tal people to the plains included the following:

i.   The traumatic experiences in the aftermath of the killing of Langkuk in 1917.
ii.   Oppressive rule of some of the chiefs in Tal like Bedung, Lafuk, and Adamu Gutus Mutkhai.
iii. Search for greener pastures and abundant fertile land different from the rocky and hilly type at home in Tal.
iv.   Traumatised by the British soldiers; bombardments, killings, and destruction of crops, houses, and several villages triggered a sudden migration of many Tal people to Shendam. Life would no longer be the same if they stayed, given the losses they suffered and the sad memory of the systematic clampdown on them by British soldiers, using sophisticated weapons. Machine guns (*maiwurwa* in Tal) would continue to torment them. After the killing of Langkuk, many people became frightened and felt unsafe, and as such, they had to move away to the plains to start a new life all over again.

v. Another push factor was the oppressive leadership style of some of the traditional chiefs of Tal. Field research revealed that many people had cause to complain during the reign of Chiefs Fotgwim and Adamu Gutus Mutkhai. For instance, some people said they had to leave Tal because of the chief's habit of forcefully taking their daughters or their wives for themselves. It was reported that once the chief declared he was interested in a woman, their aides immediately took them, usually against their consent or that of their parents, suitors, or husband, to the chief's palace to become his wife. The worst was that if anybody was seen talking to any woman who was cherished by the chief, such a person was publicly disgraced. For instance, it was alleged that a professional teacher in Tal was given a thorough beating and forced to walk naked in Balong market because it was alleged that he slept with one of the wives of Adamu Gutus Mutkhai. This act caused him to leave Tal to settle at Piapung until his death in the 1980s. In fact, many people were punished arbitrarily, whether they were guilty of the alleged offence or not, especially with regards to being seen just talking to a woman. Seizure of farmlands, bribery, and corrupt practices regarding settlement of disputes over ownership of property were very common.

vi. The desire and search for greener pasture land was a major factor. News of abundant farmland was another strong push factor responsible for the migration of the people of Tal to the plains. Hence, they wanted to move down to the plains, where very fertile farmland was in abundance and productive in the present-day Shendam, Qua'an pan, and Mikang Local Government Areas.

Apart from these factors, there were other economic and social issues that were responsible for their migration to the plains in great numbers. As noted above, farmland was readily available; opportunities for trading and sale of farm produce and livestock attracted many people to go down and settle permanently. Thus, they could earn money and stay freely with their women or families without facing any embarrassment, contrary to the case back in Tal.

The hospitable and friendly nature of the inhabitants (*indigenes*) or the host communities made things much easier. People were free to relate and socialise. Social interaction and other activities were done in an atmosphere of peace and tranquillity. There were no cases of wife seizure or forceful marriages of their daughters or women against their expressed consent.

A random movement en-masse down to the plains started around 1917. The process was unsystematic; therefore, there were no individual pioneers.

8.2 The Chronology of the Migration 1917-1970s

Movement of the Tal people was gradual and spontaneous at different times into different places and directions.

i. Some groups of people moved to the North Garram District (now in Kanke LGA), Hamtul and Kabwai, and founded Dungyel settlement.
ii. Another group of Tangge and Basnuang people moved to La'an in Pankshin District and Pankchyom and Puyhiel in Shendam Local Government Area.
iii. Vongrong (Takhong) and Kyam people moved towards the east, to Pe (Pai) and Tungkus Lalin in Mikang.
iv. Others, mainly comprising Mudong, Yong, and Kabyak, moved towards the south, to Piapung District, and founded village settlements like Gwetkat and Gotlong.
v. Mudong and Mugne people moved into Keonoem and DokaTofa settlements (now in Shendam LGA).

Today, Tal people are found in many other areas of Plateau State, such as Langtang South, Wase-Kadarko, Qua'an Pan, and Mikang. Other locations are Awe, Doma, Azara, Lafia, and Obi in Nasarawa States, and even as far as Taraba. Their movement in later life was in connection with the search for viable commercial farmlands to settle and engage in other economic/commercial activities.

8.3 The System of Land Tenure in the Plains and Political Power

Tal people were accepted just like tenants on the land. Farmland ownership belonged to their host community, especially Goemai. Farmland was usually requested for expansion or change of place; this was done through traditionally constituted authority. Initially, some men worked on farmlands as internally hired labourers and then later requested land to settle. They engaged mainly in petty trading and farming.

Having stayed for over eighty years, many Tal people have become fully integrated into the traditional community system such that now, they have a say in political power arrangements. Some have even been made village or hamlet chiefs or title holders, for exemplary conduct, thus ensuring harmonious co-existence.

8.4   Agricultural Production on the Plains

Tal people are hardworking farmers. While on the plains, they kept livestock and cultivated different types of crops: guinea corn, rice, millet, groundnuts, yam, beans, and sweet potatoes (*Khungkhung* in Tal language). Livestock kept include local chicken, goats, sheep, pigs, and cattle. Raising livestock and cultivation of commercial crops ensured great prosperity and a higher standard of living for quite a good number of people. Many of them have built modern houses and bought cars or motor vehicles, motorcycles, or bicycles to facilitate their movements or commercial means of transportation to farm or markets, hence earning extra money. This has changed the lifestyles of many of them, such that they hardly think of coming back home to settle again.

8.5   Relationship of Tal People on the Plains and Their Neighbours

As peace-loving people, highly respected for their hard work and honesty, the Tals' relationship with their neighbours has been very cordial. Because of their good human relations, hard work, and transparency, in many places they have been appointed chief. For instance, at Bada Koshi, a village settlement under Taraba, a Hamtul man, Samuel Kapkum, was appointed as the village head in the late 1990s. Under the current democratic dispensation, some of them have been elected into political offices, like councillors. For instance, during the election in 2003, Hangwai Gukyen was elected as a councillor from Tumbul ward in Langtang South. Samson Fotkom was elected as a councillor/Chief Whip in 1999 in Shendam Local Government Council.

8.6   Relationship of Tal People on the Plain with Those at Home

Most Tal people in Diaspora remain in close touch with their roots. Regular visits are made to people at home or vice versa in order to sustain the relationship that existed before their departure in search of greener pastures.

Contacts are maintained through some activities like cultural festivals (Bit Tal), marriages, funeral ceremonies, or community development association meetings that come up from time to time. Some families receive remittances in cash or kind from their members, which enables them carry out some projects like building a house or undertaking a petty trade or farm business at home.

References

Dangway, Ezekiel D. (2003). Male informant interviewed on 25/03/2003 on Tal chronology of migratory movements to the plains in Shendam; aged 82 years.

Langa, Adamu (2003). Male informant interviewed on 26/03/2003 on reasons for the migration of Tal people to the plains in Shendam, aged 90-plus years, based in Nakwan, Shendam, LGA.

Oxford Dictionary of Current English, p. 562.

Pankshin, Sabo (2011). Male informant interviewed on 14/10/2011 on World War I and World War II veterans of Tal, based in Shendam. Actual name is Sabo Guyin Yatep; age 96-plus years.

Chapter Nine

Adamu Gutus Mutkhai as Ngolong Ngas

9.1 The Creation of the Ngolong Ngas Institution

Changes of colonial administrative structures in former Pankshin Division eventually led to the creation of the stool of Ngolong Ngas, a traditional institution. Initially, up to 1953, all districts were called Native Authorities (NAs). But from 1953 to the 1960s, they were renamed Local Authorities (LAs), comprising three areas:

i.   Angas (Pankshin Division)
ii. Sura-Pyem
iii. Ron-Kulere

They were all placed under the rulership of the divisional officer (DO) at Pankshin. In 1953, a need arose for these areas to select a chief to represent them at the meeting of the House of Chiefs in Kaduna. The three areas constituted the federation recognised at that time. Given the pressing need for choosing one person, the desire then was to attempt political centralisation to ensure effective representation. Federation members welcomed this idea because all the district heads would contest among themselves to elect one person.

The person selected by this arrangement emerged from Sura-Pyem (Mangu). But Angas people rejected him. According to them, as a non-Ngas-speaking person, he was an outsider. The government then allowed Sura-Pyem and Ron-Kulere to be autonomous.

Thus Sura-Pyem and Mangu became chiefdoms. So the twelve districts of the old Pankshin Division came together and agreed to contest among themselves to select one person as the Ngolong Ngas. The outcome of this development led to the election of the first Ngolong Ngas, the late Nde Yilsu J. Dimlong, who was chosen as third class chief of Pankshin in 1953.

Adamu Gutus Mutkhai was a messenger in the provincial office in Jos before moving in the same capacity to work with the Pankshin divisional officer after his return from World War II in 1945.

9.2 The Struggle of Adamu Gutus Mutkhai to Be Elected and the Attitude of Ngas People

While working as a messenger of the divisional officer, Adamu Gutus Mutkhai had made contacts and established a good rapport with the Sardauna of Sokoto, Sir Ahmadu Bello. He also became a councillor for the Native Authority, under the platform of Northern People's Congress. He was also chairman of the same party between 1963 and 1964. He was also the chief of Tal, a position he relinquished when he was elected the Ngolong Ngas in 1965 (he was officially installed in 1967). Having taken a leadership position in party politics and local government administration, he developed an interest in traditional leadership. His exposure and experience of leadership really spurred him in the struggle towards becoming an elected traditional ruler in Pankshin Division. When the opportunity came, following the death of Nde Yilsu J. Dimlong, Adamu Gutus Mutkhai indicated interest and stood for the election. Only three people out of the twelve district heads contested the election in 1965. The results were as follows:

1.   Adamu Gutus Mutkhai from Tal District got eight votes.
2.   Haruna Gosomji Dimka from Kabwir District had one vote.
3.   Nbok Dimlong from Pankshin secured three votes.

The winner of the election was obviously clear. Adamu Gutus Mutkhai won in a land-slide victory, with eight votes out of twelve. But his victory did not go down well in the hearts of the people of Pankshin District. They did not like him and reacted violently, leading to a riot and shooting by the police, which claimed the lives of some people.

The cause of the hatred was probably connected to the killing of Chief Langkuk at the hands of his father, Mutkhai, in Tal. Their feeling was how can Adamu Gutus Mutkhai rule over them when his father was responsible for Langkuk's death? Besides, he was seen as not a pure Ngas man.

How Adamu Gutus Mutkhai escaped from the venue of the installation to his house, nobody could explain. The Angas people came out and kept vigil with bows and arrows, ready to fight, as if it were a warfare situation. The Native Authority police were sent to his house to protect him and maintain law and order.

Demonstrations of anger over the results affected his stay on the throne. Capitalising on the unfriendly atmosphere, the police commissioner, Joseph Dechi Gomwalk, used his position as governor of the Benue Plateau State and removed him. By this action, he made nonsense of the whole election processes and the final results.

Adamu Gutus Mutkhai was elected as third class traditional chief, and the staff of office was given to him by the provisional secretary, Garba Ja Abdulkadiri. During the riot, he was asked to relocate and stay at Langshi, pending the outcome of the investigation by the government on why he was removed from the throne. Members of the committee were the following:

1. Gwamna Awan (chief of Kagoro) as chairman
2. D. B. Zang, member
3. Chief of Lafiagi, member

The three-man committee completed their assignment and submitted a report to Governor Hassan Usman Katsina, who was military governor of the Northern Region. In their report, the committee did not find anything abnormal with regards to the process of electing Adamu Gutus Mutkhai as Ngolong Ngas. It was not at variance with the gazetted document of the colonial government. This investigation was before the twelve state creations of 1967. However, the release of the result of the panel coincided with the euphoria of the creation of the new state. The new governor of Benue Plateau, J. D. Gomwalk, did not act on the report sent to him from Kaduna. So while waiting for the outcome of the investigation in 1968, Adamu Gutus Mutkhai got the shock of his life: A letter came from the governor, terminating his appointment. This confirmed the grand design of his dethronement as the Ngolong Ngas. The reason stated in the letter was rather subjective. It conveyed the message that the method used in selecting him was faulty and not according to the rules and regulations. With this development, he went back to serve as the district head of Tal.

9.3   His Eventual Election as Ngolong Ngas in 1985

Adamu Gutus Mutkhai was very determined to succeed. His frustrating experience of being removed from office did not deter him from achieving his ambition to rule.

After his dethronement, the stool remained vacant, and so another arrangement was made for interested district heads to contest. For the second time, Adamu Gutus Mutkhai contested with Haruna Gosomji Dimka. They were the only two who contested. The method of voting was arbitrarily modified, as an outside councillor (Wakilin Waje) was also invited to cast votes with the twelve district heads. The results were as follows:

i.   Haruna Gosomji Dimka got twenty-one votes.
ii.   Adamu Gutus Mutkhai got seventeen votes. He lost out.

A total of thirty-eight electorates were involved. Gosomji won with twenty-one votes. Thus, he became the Ngolong Ngas in 1968. Upon the demise of Gosomji three years later, Adamu Gutus Mutkhai again contested for the seat. This time around, there were six contestants:

1.   Pius Challa Diltu
2.   Nbok Dimlong
3.   Lankang Dashwep Wale
4.   Chip Jonathan Dakrim
5.   Garram Nde Yilji
6.   Adamu Gutus Mutkhai

The normal voting procedure was adopted for the election; councillors were excluded. The results were as follow:

i.   Pius C. Diltu: four votes
ii.   Nbok Dimlong: four votes
iii. L. Dashwep Wale: one vote

iv.   C. Jonathan Dakrim: one vote

v.   G. Nde Yilji: one vote

vi.   Adamu Gutus Mutkhai: one vote

Because of the tie, another round of voting was organised for the two candidates who had four votes each. In the second round of voting, Pius Diltu had seven votes and Nbok Dimlong pulled five votes. Thus, Pius C. Diltu won and was installed as the Ngolong Ngas in 1979.

However, in 1983, when Pius C. Diltu died, Adamu Gutus Mutkhai again entered the contest for the fourth time, with Nbok Dimlong. Only the twelve district heads were allowed to cast votes among themselves to select one person. The result of the voting showed that both candidates had six votes each. The vote was repeated, and for the second time, it was a tie. So a slight modification was adopted: lucky-dip. The two names, Nbok and Gutus, were written down, and the winner would be picked by the electoral officer. Nbok Dimlong's name was picked, so he won the election and became the Ngolong Ngas.

HRH Adamu Gutus Mutkhai
Late Ngolong, Ngas (1985-1995) Pankshin LGA

Figure 9.1: Adamu Gutus Mutkhai

Nbok Dimlong ruled for only six months, and then he died. The vacuum had to be filled again. Two people indicated their interest to contest. Adamu Gutus Mutkhai, for the fifth time, was one of them. The other contestant was Joshua Dimlong, of Pankshin District.

Voting was done by the twelve heads, and the result was as follows:

i.   Adamu Gutus Mutkhai: six votes
ii.   Joshua Dimlong: six votes

It was a tie. Twice it was repeated, and twice it was a tie. So the lucky-dip method was used to determine the winner. When the paper was picked, it bore the name of Adamu Gutus Mutkhai. He was finally elected and installed as Ngolong Ngas in 1985.

The conduct of the election was authorised by General Chris Mohammed Ali (Rtd.). Presentation of the staff of office, which was upgraded to first class status, was done by Colonel Lawrence Anebi Onoja, military governor of Plateau State, on 21/3/1987.

Adamu Gutus Mutkhai (figure 9.1) was the first recipient, as first class paramount ruler on the throne of Ngolong Ngas, in Pankshin Local Government Area.

While on the throne, he distinguished himself as a model by dint of hard work as a traditional ruler. His outstanding performance earned him a number of prestigious awards from reputable organisations in Nigeria. In fact, he was the first recipient of such awards in the history of the local government. These awards included the following:

i.   Qualified and Incorporated Administrative Manager (QIAM)
ii.   Institute's Highest Award of Honorary Fellowship (FIAM)
iii. Certified and Distinguished Traditional Administrator (CDTA)

Most of these awards came from the Institute of Administrative Management in Nigeria certificate of award scheme.

Adamu Gutus Mutkhai, at his time, was the longest serving traditional ruler in Pankshin Local Government. He ruled for ten years, from August 1985 to 1995. He died in Pankshin.

References

Charles, Jacob C. (1993-1994). Interviewed on Adamu Gutus Mutkhai and Ngolong Ngas.

Mutkhai, Adamu Gutus (1994). Interviewed on 04/09/1994.

Plateau State Government Gazette (1978). Appointment and Deposition of Chiefs (Appointment of Chief of Angas) Order, 1978.